The Coming Race

by

Edward Bulwer, Lord Lytton

The Coming Race
by Edward Bulwer, Lord Lytton

Copyright © 2023

All Rights reserved.
No part of this publication may be reproduced, stored in a retrieval system, or transmitted in any form or by any means, electronic, mechanical, photocopying or Otherwise, without the written permission of the publisher.

The author/editor asserts the moral right to be identified as the author/editor of this work.

ISBN: 978-93-57276-66-5

Published by

DOUBLE 9 BOOKS

2/13-B, Ansari Road
Daryaganj, New Delhi – 110002
info@double9books.com
www.double9books.com
Tel. 011-40042856

This book is under public domain

ABOUT THE AUTHOR

Edward Bulwer Lord Lytton, 1st Baron Lytton, PC (25 May 1803 – 18 January 1873) was an English writer and politician. From 1831 to 1841, he was a Whig in the House of Commons, and from 1851 to 1866, he was a Conservative. Between June 1858 until June 1859, while serving as Secretary of State for the Colonies, he selected Richard Clement Moody as the first premier of British Columbia. Following King Otto's abdication in 1862, he turned down the Greek Crown. In 1866, he was made Baron Lytton of Knebworth. His works were favorably received and made Bulwer-Lytton wealthy. In addition to the opening line "It was a dark and stormy night," he also coined terms like "the great unwashed," "pursuit of the almighty dollar," "the pen is mightier than the sword," and "dweller on the threshold." Since 1982, the satirical Bulwer-Lytton Fiction Contest has purportedly sought the "first sentence of the poorest of all imaginable novels." General William Earle Bulwer of Heydon Hall and Wood Dalling, Norfolk, and Elizabeth Barbara Lytton, a descendant of Richard Warburton Lytton of Knebworth House, Hertfordshire, welcomed Bulwer into the world on May 25, 1803. William Earle Lytton Bulwer (1799–1877) and Henry (1801–1872), who would eventually become Lord Dalling and Bulwer, were his two older brothers.

CONTENTS

Chapter I. 7

Chapter II. 10

Chapter III. 12

Chapter IV. 14

Chapter V. 16

Chapter VI. 24

Chapter VII. 25

Chapter VIII. 31

Chapter IX. 32

Chapter X. 40

Chapter XI. 44

Chapter XII. 46

Chapter XIII. 52

Chapter XIV. 54

Chapter XV. 57

Chapter XVI. 65

Chapter XVII. 74

Chapter XVIII. 84

Chapter XIX. 92

Chapter XX. 94

Chapter XXI. 97

Chapter XXII. 100

Chapter XXIII. 106

Chapter XXIV. 114

Chapter XXV. 116

Chapter XXVI. 130

Chapter XXVII. 136

Chapter XXVIII. 139

Chapter XXIX. 142

Chapter I.

I am a native of ____, in the United States of America. My ancestors migrated from England in the reign of Charles II.; and my grandfather was not undistinguished in the War of Independence. My family, therefore, enjoyed a somewhat high social position in right of birth; and being also opulent, they were considered disqualified for the public service. My father once ran for Congress, but was signally defeated by his tailor. After that event he interfered little in politics, and lived much in his library. I was the eldest of three sons, and sent at the age of sixteen to the old country, partly to complete my literary education, partly to commence my commercial training in a mercantile firm at Liverpool. My father died shortly after I was twenty-one; and being left well off, and having a taste for travel and adventure, I resigned, for a time, all pursuit of the almighty dollar, and became a desultory wanderer over the face of the earth.

In the year 18__, happening to be in ____, I was invited by a professional engineer, with whom I had made acquaintance, to visit the recesses of the _____ mine, upon which he was employed.

The reader will understand, ere he close this narrative, my reason for concealing all clue to the district of which I write, and will perhaps thank me for refraining from any description that may tend to its discovery.

Let me say, then, as briefly as possible, that I accompanied the engineer into the interior of the mine, and became so strangely fascinated by its gloomy wonders, and so interested in my friend's explorations, that I prolonged my stay in the neighbourhood, and descended daily, for some weeks, into the vaults and galleries hollowed by nature and art beneath the surface of the earth. The engineer was persuaded that far richer deposits of mineral wealth than had yet been detected, would be found in a new shaft that had been commenced under his operations. In piercing this shaft we came one day upon a chasm jagged and seemingly charred at the sides, as if burst asunder at some distant period by volcanic fires. Down this chasm my friend caused himself to be lowered in a 'cage,' having first tested the atmosphere by the safety-lamp. He remained nearly an hour in the abyss. When he returned he was very pale, and with an anxious, thoughtful expression of face, very different from its ordinary character, which was open, cheerful, and fearless.

He said briefly that the descent appeared to him unsafe, and leading to no result; and, suspending further operations in the shaft, we returned to the more familiar parts of the mine.

All the rest of that day the engineer seemed preoccupied by some absorbing thought. He was unusually taciturn, and there was a scared, bewildered look in his eyes, as that of a man who has seen a ghost. At night, as we two were sitting alone in the lodging we shared together near the mouth of the mine, I said to my friend,—

"Tell me frankly what you saw in that chasm: I am sure it was something strange and terrible. Whatever it be, it has left your mind in a state of doubt. In such a case two heads are better than one. Confide in me."

The engineer long endeavoured to evade my inquiries; but as, while he spoke, he helped himself unconsciously out of the brandy-flask to a degree to which he was wholly unaccustomed, for he was a very temperate man, his reserve gradually melted away. He who would keep himself to himself should imitate the dumb animals, and drink water. At last he said, "I will tell you all. When the cage stopped, I found myself on a ridge of rock; and below me, the chasm, taking a slanting direction, shot down to a considerable depth, the darkness of which my lamp could not have penetrated. But through it, to my infinite surprise, streamed upward a steady brilliant light. Could it be any volcanic fire? In that case, surely I should have felt the heat. Still, if on this there was doubt, it was of the utmost importance to our common safety to clear it up. I examined the sides of the descent, and found that I could venture to trust myself to the irregular projection of ledges, at least for some way. I left the cage and clambered down. As I drew nearer and nearer to the light, the chasm became wider, and at last I saw, to my unspeakable amaze, a broad level road at the bottom of the abyss, illumined as far as the eye could reach by what seemed artificial gas-lamps placed at regular intervals, as in the thoroughfare of a great city; and I heard confusedly at a distance a hum as of human voices. I know, of course, that no rival miners are at work in this district. Whose could be those voices? What human hands could have levelled that road and marshalled those lamps?

"The superstitious belief, common to miners, that gnomes or fiends dwell within the bowels of the earth, began to seize me. I shuddered at the thought of descending further and braving the inhabitants of this nether valley. Nor indeed could I have done so without ropes, as from the spot I had reached to the bottom of the chasm the sides of the rock sank down abrupt, smooth, and sheer. I retraced my steps with some difficulty. Now I have told you all."

"You will descend again?"

"I ought, yet I feel as if I durst not."

"A trusty companion halves the journey and doubles the courage. I will go with you. We will provide ourselves with ropes of suitable length and strength—and—pardon me—you must not drink more tonight, our hands and feet must be steady and firm tomorrow."

Chapter II.

With the morning my friend's nerves were rebraced, and he was not less excited by curiosity than myself. Perhaps more; for he evidently believed in his own story, and I felt considerable doubt of it; not that he would have wilfully told an untruth, but that I thought he must have been under one of those hallucinations which seize on our fancy or our nerves in solitary, unaccustomed places, and in which we give shape to the formless and sound to the dumb.

We selected six veteran miners to watch our descent; and as the cage held only one at a time, the engineer descended first; and when he had gained the ledge at which he had before halted, the cage rearose for me. I soon gained his side. We had provided ourselves with a strong coil of rope.

The light struck on my sight as it had done the day before on my friend's. The hollow through which it came sloped diagonally: it seemed to me a diffused atmospheric light, not like that from fire, but soft and silvery, as from a northern star. Quitting the cage, we descended, one after the other, easily enough, owing to the juts in the side, till we reached the place at which my friend had previously halted, and which was a projection just spacious enough to allow us to stand abreast. From this spot the chasm widened rapidly like the lower end of a vast funnel, and I saw distinctly the valley, the road, the lamps which my companion had described. He had exaggerated nothing. I heard the sounds he had heard—a mingled indescribable hum as of voices and a dull tramp as of feet. Straining my eye farther down, I clearly beheld at a distance the outline of some large building. It could not be mere natural rock, it was too symmetrical, with huge heavy Egyptian-like columns, and the whole lighted as from within. I had about me a small pocket-telescope, and by the aid of this, I could distinguish, near the building I mention, two forms which seemed human, though I could not be sure. At least they were living, for they moved, and both vanished within the building. We now proceeded to attach the end of the rope we had brought with us to the ledge on which we stood, by the aid of clamps and grappling hooks, with which, as well as with necessary tools, we were provided.

We were almost silent in our work. We toiled like men afraid to speak to each other. One end of the rope being thus apparently made firm to the ledge, the other, to which we fastened a fragment of the rock, rested on the ground below, a distance of some fifty feet. I was a younger man and a more active man than my companion, and having served on board ship in my boyhood, this mode of transit was more familiar to me than to him. In a whisper I claimed the precedence, so that when I gained the ground I might serve to hold the rope more steady for his descent. I got safely to the ground beneath, and the engineer now began to lower himself. But he had scarcely accomplished ten feet of the descent, when the fastenings, which we had fancied so secure, gave way, or rather the rock itself proved treacherous and crumbled beneath the strain; and the unhappy man was precipitated to the bottom, falling just at my feet, and bringing down with his fall splinters of the rock, one of which, fortunately but a small one, struck and for the time stunned me. When I recovered my senses I saw my companion an inanimate mass beside me, life utterly extinct. While I was bending over his corpse in grief and horror, I heard close at hand a strange sound between a snort and a hiss; and turning instinctively to the quarter from which it came, I saw emerging from a dark fissure in the rock a vast and terrible head, with open jaws and dull, ghastly, hungry eyes—the head of a monstrous reptile resembling that of the crocodile or alligator, but infinitely larger than the largest creature of that kind I had ever beheld in my travels. I started to my feet and fled down the valley at my utmost speed. I stopped at last, ashamed of my panic and my flight, and returned to the spot on which I had left the body of my friend. It was gone; doubtless the monster had already drawn it into its den and devoured it. The rope and the grappling-hooks still lay where they had fallen, but they afforded me no chance of return; it was impossible to re-attach them to the rock above, and the sides of the rock were too sheer and smooth for human steps to clamber. I was alone in this strange world, amidst the bowels of the earth.

Chapter III.

Slowly and cautiously I went my solitary way down the lamplit road and towards the large building I have described. The road itself seemed like a great Alpine pass, skirting rocky mountains of which the one through whose chasm I had descended formed a link. Deep below to the left lay a vast valley, which presented to my astonished eye the unmistakeable evidences of art and culture. There were fields covered with a strange vegetation, similar to none I have seen above the earth; the colour of it not green, but rather of a dull and leaden hue or of a golden red.

There were lakes and rivulets which seemed to have been curved into artificial banks; some of pure water, others that shone like pools of naphtha. At my right hand, ravines and defiles opened amidst the rocks, with passes between, evidently constructed by art, and bordered by trees resembling, for the most part, gigantic ferns, with exquisite varieties of feathery foliage, and stems like those of the palm-tree. Others were more like the cane-plant, but taller, bearing large clusters of flowers. Others, again, had the form of enormous fungi, with short thick stems supporting a wide dome-like roof, from which either rose or drooped long slender branches. The whole scene behind, before, and beside me far as the eye could reach, was brilliant with innumerable lamps. The world without a sun was bright and warm as an Italian landscape at noon, but the air less oppressive, the heat softer. Nor was the scene before me void of signs of habitation. I could distinguish at a distance, whether on the banks of the lake or rivulet, or half-way upon eminences, embedded amidst the vegetation, buildings that must surely be the homes of men. I could even discover, though far off, forms that appeared to me human moving amidst the landscape. As I paused to gaze, I saw to the right, gliding quickly through the air, what appeared a small boat, impelled by sails shaped like wings. It soon passed out of sight, descending amidst the shades of a forest. Right above me there was no sky, but only a cavernous roof. This roof grew higher and higher at the distance of the landscapes beyond, till it became imperceptible, as an atmosphere of haze formed itself beneath.

Continuing my walk, I started,—from a bush that resembled a great tangle of sea-weeds, interspersed with fern-like shrubs and plants of large leafage shaped like that of the aloe or prickly-pear,—a curious animal about the size and shape of a deer. But as, after bounding away a few paces, it turned round and gazed at me inquisitively, I perceived that it was not like any species of deer now extant above the earth, but it brought instantly to my recollection a plaster cast I had seen in some museum of a variety of the elk stag, said to have existed before the Deluge. The creature seemed tame enough, and, after inspecting me a moment or two, began to graze on the singular herbiage around undismayed and careless.

Chapter IV.

I now came in full sight of the building. Yes, it had been made by hands, and hollowed partly out of a great rock. I should have supposed it at the first glance to have been of the earliest form of Egyptian architecture. It was fronted by huge columns, tapering upward from massive plinths, and with capitals that, as I came nearer, I perceived to be more ornamental and more fantastically graceful that Egyptian architecture allows. As the Corinthian capital mimics the leaf of the acanthus, so the capitals of these columns imitated the foliage of the vegetation neighbouring them, some aloe-like, some fern-like. And now there came out of this building a form—human;— was it human? It stood on the broad way and looked around, beheld me and approached. It came within a few yards of me, and at the sight and presence of it an indescribable awe and tremor seized me, rooting my feet to the ground. It reminded me of symbolical images of Genius or Demon that are seen on Etruscan vases or limned on the walls of Eastern sepulchres—images that borrow the outlines of man, and are yet of another race. It was tall, not gigantic, but tall as the tallest man below the height of giants.

Its chief covering seemed to me to be composed of large wings folded over its breast and reaching to its knees; the rest of its attire was composed of an under tunic and leggings of some thin fibrous material. It wore on its head a kind of tiara that shone with jewels, and carried in its right hand a slender staff of bright metal like polished steel. But the face! it was that which inspired my awe and my terror. It was the face of man, but yet of a type of man distinct from our known extant races. The nearest approach to it in outline and expression is the face of the sculptured sphinx—so regular in its calm, intellectual, mysterious beauty. Its colour was peculiar, more like that of the red man than any other variety of our species, and yet different from it—a richer and a softer hue, with large black eyes, deep and brilliant, and brows arched as a semicircle. The face was beardless; but a nameless something in the aspect, tranquil though the expression, and beauteous though the features, roused that instinct of danger which the sight of a tiger or serpent arouses. I felt that this manlike image was endowed with forces inimical to man. As it drew near, a cold shudder came over me. I fell on my knees and covered my face with my hands.

Chapter V.

A voice accosted me—a very quiet and very musical key of voice—in a language of which I could not understand a word, but it served to dispel my fear. I uncovered my face and looked up. The stranger (I could scarcely bring myself to call him man) surveyed me with an eye that seemed to read to the very depths of my heart. He then placed his left hand on my forehead, and with the staff in his right, gently touched my shoulder. The effect of this double contact was magical. In place of my former terror there passed into me a sense of contentment, of joy, of confidence in myself and in the being before me. I rose and spoke in my own language. He listened to me with apparent attention, but with a slight surprise in his looks; and shook his head, as if to signify that I was not understood. He then took me by the hand and led me in silence to the building. The entrance was open—indeed there was no door to it. We entered an immense hall, lighted by the same kind of lustre as in the scene without, but diffusing a fragrant odour. The floor was in large tesselated blocks of precious metals, and partly covered with a sort of matlike carpeting. A strain of low music, above and around, undulated as if from invisible instruments, seeming to belong naturally to the place, just as the sound of murmuring waters belongs to a rocky landscape, or the warble of birds to vernal groves.

A figure in a simpler garb than that of my guide, but of similar fashion, was standing motionless near the threshold. My guide touched it twice with his staff, and it put itself into a rapid and gliding movement, skimming noiselessly over the floor. Gazing on it, I then saw that it was no living form, but a mechanical automaton. It might be two minutes after it vanished through a doorless opening, half screened by curtains at the other end of the hall, when through the same opening advanced a boy of about twelve years old, with features closely resembling those of my guide, so that they seemed to me evidently son and father. On seeing me the child uttered a cry, and lifted a staff like that borne by my guide, as if in menace.

At a word from the elder he dropped it. The two then conversed for some moments, examining me while they spoke. The child touched my garments, and stroked my face with evident curiosity, uttering a sound like a laugh, but with an hilarity more subdued that the mirth of our laughter. Presently the roof of the hall opened, and a platform descended, seemingly constructed on the same principle as the 'lifts' used in hotels and warehouses for mounting from one story to another.

The stranger placed himself and the child on the platform, and motioned to me to do the same, which I did. We ascended quickly and safely, and alighted in the midst of a corridor with doorways on either side.

Through one of these doorways I was conducted into a chamber fitted up with an oriental splendour; the walls were tesselated with spars, and metals, and uncut jewels; cushions and divans abounded; apertures as for windows but unglazed, were made in the chamber opening to the floor; and as I passed along I observed that these openings led into spacious balconies, and commanded views of the illumined landscape without. In cages suspended from the ceiling there were birds of strange form and bright plumage, which at our entrance set up a chorus of song, modulated into tune as is that of our piping bullfinches. A delicious fragrance, from censers of gold elaborately sculptured, filled the air. Several automata, like the one I had seen, stood dumb and motionless by the walls. The stranger placed me beside him on a divan and again spoke to me, and again I spoke, but without the least advance towards understanding each other.

But now I began to feel the effects of the blow I had received from the splinters of the falling rock more acutely that I had done at first.

There came over me a sense of sickly faintness, accompanied with acute, lancinating pains in the head and neck. I sank back on the seat and strove in vain to stifle a groan. On this the child, who had hitherto seemed to eye me with distrust or dislike, knelt by my side to support me; taking one of my hands in both his own, he approached his lips to my forehead, breathing on it softly. In a few moments my pain ceased; a drowsy, heavy calm crept over me; I fell asleep.

How long I remained in this state I know not, but when I woke I felt perfectly restored. My eyes opened upon a group of silent forms, seated around me in the gravity and quietude of Orientals—all more or less like the first stranger; the same mantling wings, the same fashion of garment, the same sphinx-like faces, with the deep dark eyes and red man's colour; above all, the same type of race—race akin to man's, but infinitely stronger of form and grandeur of aspect—and inspiring the same unutterable feeling of dread. Yet each countenance was mild and tranquil, and even kindly in expression. And, strangely enough, it seemed to me that in this very calm and benignity consisted the secret of the dread which the countenances inspired. They seemed as void of the lines and shadows which care and sorrow, and passion and sin, leave upon the faces of men, as are the faces of sculptured gods, or as, in the eyes of Christian mourners, seem the peaceful brows of the dead.

I felt a warm hand on my shoulder; it was the child's. In his eyes there was a sort of lofty pity and tenderness, such as that with which we may gaze on some suffering bird or butterfly. I shrank from that touch—I shrank from that eye. I was vaguely impressed with a belief that, had he so pleased, that child could have killed me as easily as a man can kill a bird or a butterfly. The child seemed pained at my repugnance, quitted me, and placed himself beside one of the windows. The others continued to converse with each other in a low tone, and by their glances towards me I could perceive that I was the object of their conversation. One in especial seemed to be urging some proposal affecting me on the being whom I had first met, and this last by his gesture seemed about to assent to it, when the child suddenly quitted his post by the window, placed himself between me and the other forms, as if in protection, and spoke quickly and eagerly. By some intuition or instinct I felt that the child I had before so dreaded was pleading in my behalf. Ere he had ceased another stranger entered the room. He appeared older than the rest, though not old; his countenance less smoothly serene than theirs, though equally regular in its features, seemed to me to have more the touch of a humanity akin to my own. He listened quietly to the words addressed to him, first by my guide, next by two others of the group, and lastly by the child; then turned towards myself, and addressed me, not by words, but by signs and gestures. These I fancied that I perfectly understood, and I was not mistaken. I comprehended that he inquired whence I came. I extended my arm, and pointed towards the road which had led me from the chasm in the rock; then an idea seized me. I drew forth my pocket-book, and sketched on one of its blank leaves a rough design of the ledge of the rock, the rope, myself clinging to it; then of the cavernous rock below, the head of the reptile, the lifeless form of my friend. I gave this primitive kind of hieroglyph to my interrogator, who, after inspecting it gravely, handed it to his next neighbour, and it thus passed round the group. The being I had at first encountered then said a few words, and the child, who approached and looked at my drawing, nodded as if he comprehended its purport, and, returning to the window, expanded the wings attached to his form, shook them once or twice, and then launched himself into space without. I started up in amaze and hastened to the window. The child was already in the air, buoyed on his wings, which he did not flap to and fro as a bird does, but which were elevated over his head, and seemed to bear him steadily aloft without effort of his own. His flight seemed as swift as an eagle's; and I observed that it was towards the rock whence I had descended, of which the outline loomed visible in the brilliant atmosphere. In a very few minutes he returned, skimming through the opening from which he had gone, and dropping on the floor the rope and grappling-hooks I had left at the descent from the chasm. Some words in a low tone passed between the being present; one of the group touched an automaton, which started forward and glided from the room; then the last comer, who had addressed me by gestures, rose, took me by the hand, and led me into the corridor. There the platform by which I had mounted awaited us; we placed ourselves on it and were lowered into the hall below. My new companion, still holding me by the hand, conducted me from the building into a street (so to speak) that stretched beyond it, with buildings on either side, separated from each other by gardens bright with rich-coloured vegetation and strange flowers. Interspersed amidst these gardens, which were divided from each other by low walls, or walking slowly along the road, were many forms similar to those I had already seen. Some of the passers-by, on observing me, approached my guide, evidently by their tones, looks, and gestures addressing to him inquiries about myself. In a few moments a crowd collected around us, examining me with great interest, as if I were some rare wild animal. Yet even in gratifying their curiosity they preserved a grave and courteous demeanour; and after a few words from my guide, who seemed to me to deprecate obstruction in our road, they fell back with a stately inclination of head, and resumed their own way with tranquil indifference. Midway in this thoroughfare we stopped at a building that differed from those we had hitherto passed, inasmuch as it formed three sides of a vast court, at the angles of which were lofty pyramidal towers; in the open space between the sides was a circular fountain of colossal dimensions, and throwing up a dazzling spray of what seemed to me fire. We entered the building through an open doorway and came into an enormous hall, in which were several groups of children, all apparently employed in work as at some great factory. There was a huge engine in the wall which was in full play, with wheels and cylinders resembling our own steam-engines, except that it was richly ornamented with precious stones and metals, and appeared to emanate a pale phosphorescent atmosphere of shifting light. Many of the children were at some mysterious work on this machinery, others were seated before tables. I was not allowed to linger long enough to examine into the nature of their employment. Not one young voice was heard—not one young face turned to gaze on us. They were all still and indifferent as may be ghosts, through the midst of which pass unnoticed the forms of the living.

Quitting this hall, my guide led me through a gallery richly painted in compartments, with a barbaric mixture of gold in the colours, like pictures by Louis Cranach. The subjects described on these walls appeared to my glance as intended to illustrate events in the history of the race amidst which I was admitted. In all there were figures, most of them like the manlike creatures I had seen, but not all in the same fashion of garb, nor all with wings. There were also the effigies of various animals and birds, wholly strange to me, with backgrounds depicting landscapes or buildings. So far as my imperfect knowledge of the pictorial art would allow me to form an opinion, these paintings seemed very accurate in design and very rich in colouring, showing a perfect knowledge of perspective, but their details not arranged according to the rules of composition acknowledged by our artists—wanting, as it were, a centre; so that the effect was vague, scattered, confused, bewildering—they were like heterogeneous fragments of a dream of art.

We now came into a room of moderate size, in which was assembled what I afterwards knew to be the family of my guide, seated at a table spread as for repast. The forms thus grouped were those of my guide's wife, his daughter, and two sons. I recognised at once the difference between the two sexes, though the two females were of taller stature and ampler proportions than the males; and their countenances, if still more symmetrical in outline and contour, were devoid of the softness and timidity of expression which give charm to the face of woman as seen on the earth above. The wife wore no wings, the daughter wore wings longer than those of the males.

My guide uttered a few words, on which all the persons seated rose, and with that peculiar mildness of look and manner which I have before noticed, and which is, in truth, the common attribute of this formidable race, they saluted me according to their fashion, which consists in laying the right hand very gently on the head and uttering a soft sibilant monosyllable—S.Si, equivalent to "Welcome."

The mistress of the house then seated me beside her, and heaped a golden platter before me from one of the dishes.

While I ate (and though the viands were new to me, I marvelled more at the delicacy than the strangeness of their flavour), my companions conversed quietly, and, so far as I could detect, with polite avoidance of any direct reference to myself, or any obtrusive scrutiny of my appearance. Yet I was the first creature of that variety of the human race to which I belong that they had ever beheld, and was consequently regarded by them as a most curious and abnormal phenomenon. But all rudeness is unknown to this people, and the youngest child is taught to despise any vehement emotional demonstration. When the meal was ended, my guide again took me by the hand, and, re-entering the gallery, touched a metallic plate inscribed with strange figures, and which I rightly conjectured to be of the nature of our telegraphs. A platform descended, but this time we mounted to a much greater height than in the former building, and found ourselves in a room of moderate dimensions, and which in its general character had much that might be familiar to the associations of a visitor from the upper world. There were shelves on the wall containing what appeared to be books, and indeed were so; mostly very small, like our diamond duodecimos, shaped in the fashion of our volumes, and bound in sheets of fine metal. There were several curious-looking pieces of mechanism scattered about, apparently models, such as might be seen in the study of any professional mechanician. Four automata (mechanical contrivances which, with these people, answer the ordinary purposes of domestic service) stood phantom-like at each angle in the wall. In a recess was a low couch, or bed with pillows. A window, with curtains of some fibrous material drawn aside, opened upon a large balcony. My host stepped out into the balcony; I followed him. We were on the uppermost story of one of the angular pyramids; the view beyond was of a wild and solemn beauty impossible to describe:—the vast ranges of precipitous rock which formed the distant background, the intermediate valleys of mystic many-coloured herbiage, the flash of waters, many of them like streams of roseate flame, the serene lustre diffused over all by myriads of lamps, combined to form a whole of which no words of mine can convey adequate description; so splendid was it, yet so sombre; so lovely, yet so awful.

But my attention was soon diverted from these nether landscapes. Suddenly there arose, as from the streets below, a burst of joyous music; then a winged form soared into the space; another as if in chase of the first, another and another; others after others, till the crowd grew thick and the number countless. But how describe the fantastic grace of these forms in their undulating movements! They appeared engaged in some sport or amusement; now forming into opposite squadrons; now scattering; now each group threading the other, soaring, descending, interweaving, severing; all in measured time to the music below, as if in the dance of the fabled Peri.

I turned my gaze on my host in a feverish wonder. I ventured to place my hand on the large wings that lay folded on his breast, and in doing so a slight shock as of electricity passed through me. I recoiled in fear; my host smiled, and as if courteously to gratify my curiosity, slowly expanded his pinions. I observed that his garment beneath them became dilated as a bladder that fills with air. The arms seemed to slide into the wings, and in another moment he had launched himself into the luminous atmosphere, and hovered there, still, and with outspread wings, as an eagle that basks in the sun. Then, rapidly as an eagle swoops, he rushed downwards into the midst of one of the groups, skimming through the midst, and as suddenly again soaring aloft. Thereon, three forms, in one of which I thought to recognise my host's daughter, detached themselves from the rest, and followed him as a bird sportively follows a bird. My eyes, dazzled with the lights and bewildered by the throngs, ceased to distinguish the gyrations and evolutions of these winged playmates, till presently my host re-emerged from the crowd and alighted at my side.

The strangeness of all I had seen began now to operate fast on my senses; my mind itself began to wander. Though not inclined to be superstitious, nor hitherto believing that man could be brought into bodily communication with demons, I felt the terror and the wild excitement with which, in the Gothic ages, a traveller might have persuaded himself that he witnessed a 'sabbat' of fiends and witches. I have a vague recollection of having attempted with vehement gesticulation, and forms of exorcism, and loud incoherent words, to repel my courteous and indulgent host; of his mild endeavors to calm and soothe me; of his intelligent conjecture that my fright and bewilderment were occasioned by the difference of form and movement between us which the wings that had excited my marvelling curiosity had, in exercise, made still more strongly perceptible; of the gentle smile with which he had sought to dispel my alarm by dropping the wings to the ground and endeavouring to show me that they were but a mechanical contrivance. That sudden transformation did but increase my horror, and as extreme fright often shows itself by extreme daring, I sprang at his throat like a wild beast. On an instant I was felled to the ground as by an electric shock, and the last confused images floating before my sight ere I became wholly insensible, were the form of my host kneeling beside me with one hand on my forehead, and the beautiful calm face of his daughter, with large, deep, inscrutable eyes intently fixed upon my own.

Chapter VI.

I remained in this unconscious state, as I afterwards learned, for many days, even for some weeks according to our computation of time. When I recovered I was in a strange room, my host and all his family were gathered round me, and to my utter amaze my host's daughter accosted me in my own language with a slightly foreign accent.

"How do you feel?" she asked.

It was some moments before I could overcome my surprise enough to falter out, "You know my language? How? Who and what are you?"

My host smiled and motioned to one of his sons, who then took from a table a number of thin metallic sheets on which were traced drawings of various figures—a house, a tree, a bird, a man, &c.

In these designs I recognised my own style of drawing. Under each figure was written the name of it in my language, and in my writing; and in another handwriting a word strange to me beneath it.

Said the host, "Thus we began; and my daughter Zee, who belongs to the College of Sages, has been your instructress and ours too."

Zee then placed before me other metallic sheets, on which, in my writing, words first, and then sentences, were inscribed. Under each word and each sentence strange characters in another hand. Rallying my senses, I comprehended that thus a rude dictionary had been effected. Had it been done while I was dreaming? "That is enough now," said Zee, in a tone of command. "Repose and take food."

Chapter VII.

A room to myself was assigned to me in this vast edifice. It was prettily and fantastically arranged, but without any of the splendour of metal-work or gems which was displayed in the more public apartments. The walls were hung with a variegated matting made from the stalks and fibers of plants, and the floor carpeted with the same.

The bed was without curtains, its supports of iron resting on balls of crystal; the coverings, of a thin white substance resembling cotton. There were sundry shelves containing books. A curtained recess communicated with an aviary filled with singing-birds, of which I did not recognise one resembling those I have seen on earth, except a beautiful species of dove, though this was distinguished from our doves by a tall crest of bluish plumes. All these birds had been trained to sing in artful tunes, and greatly exceeded the skill of our piping bullfinches, which can rarely achieve more than two tunes, and cannot, I believe, sing those in concert. One might have supposed one's self at an opera in listening to the voices in my aviary. There were duets and trios, and quartetts and choruses, all arranged as in one piece of music. Did I want silence from the birds? I had but to draw a curtain over the aviary, and their song hushed as they found themselves left in the dark. Another opening formed a window, not glazed, but on touching a spring, a shutter ascended from the floor, formed of some substance less transparent than glass, but still sufficiently pellucid to allow a softened view of the scene without. To this window was attached a balcony, or rather hanging garden, wherein grew many graceful plants and brilliant flowers. The apartment and its appurtenances had thus a character, if strange in detail, still familiar, as a whole, to modern notions of luxury, and would have excited admiration if found attached to the apartments of an English duchess or a fashionable French author. Before I arrived this was Zee's chamber; she had hospitably assigned it to me.

Some hours after the waking up which is described in my last chapter, I was lying alone on my couch trying to fix my thoughts on conjecture as to the nature and genus of the people amongst whom I was thrown, when my host and his daughter Zee entered the room. My host, still speaking my native language, inquired with much politeness, whether it would be agreeable to me to converse, or if I preferred solitude. I replied, that I should feel much honoured and obliged by the opportunity offered me to express my gratitude for the hospitality and civilities I had received in a country to which I was a stranger, and to learn enough of its customs and manners not to offend through ignorance.

As I spoke, I had of course risen from my couch: but Zee, much to my confusion, curtly ordered me to lie down again, and there was something in her voice and eye, gentle as both were, that compelled my obedience. She then seated herself unconcernedly at the foot of my bed, while her father took his place on a divan a few feet distant.

"But what part of the world do you come from?" asked my host, "that we should appear so strange to you and you to us? I have seen individual specimens of nearly all the races differing from our own, except the primeval savages who dwell in the most desolate and remote recesses of uncultivated nature, unacquainted with other light than that they obtain from volcanic fires, and contented to grope their way in the dark, as do many creeping, crawling and flying things. But certainly you cannot be a member of those barbarous tribes, nor, on the other hand, do you seem to belong to any civilised people."

I was somewhat nettled at this last observation, and replied that I had the honour to belong to one of the most civilised nations of the earth; and that, so far as light was concerned, while I admired the ingenuity and disregard of expense with which my host and his fellow-citizens had contrived to illumine the regions unpenetrated by the rays of the sun, yet I could not conceive how any who had once beheld the orbs of heaven could compare to their lustre the artificial lights invented by the necessities of man. But my host said he had seen specimens of most of the races differing from his own, save the wretched barbarians he had mentioned. Now, was it possible that he had never been on the surface of the earth, or could he only be referring to communities buried within its entrails?

My host was for some moments silent; his countenance showed a degree of surprise which the people of that race very rarely manifest under any circumstances, howsoever extraordinary. But Zee was more intelligent, and exclaimed, "So you see, my father, that there is truth in the old tradition; there always is truth in every tradition commonly believed in all times and by all tribes."

"Zee," said my host mildly, "you belong to the College of Sages, and ought to be wiser than I am; but, as chief of the Light-preserving Council, it is my duty to take nothing for granted till it is proved to the evidence of my own senses." Then, turning to me, he asked me several questions about the surface of the earth and the heavenly bodies; upon which, though I answered him to the best of my knowledge, my answers seemed not to satisfy nor convince him. He shook his head quietly, and, changing the subject rather abruptly, asked how I had come down from what he was pleased to call one world to the other. I answered, that under the surface of the earth there were mines containing minerals, or metals, essential to our wants and our progress in all arts and industries; and I then briefly explained the manner in which, while exploring one of those mines, I and my ill-fated friend had obtained a glimpse of the regions into which we had descended, and how the descent had cost him his life; appealing to the rope and grappling-hooks that the child had brought to the house in which I had been at first received, as a witness of the truthfulness of my story.

My host then proceeded to question me as to the habits and modes of life among the races on the upper earth, more especially among those considered to be the most advanced in that civilisation which he was pleased to define "the art of diffusing throughout a community the tranquil happiness which belongs to a virtuous and well-ordered household." Naturally desiring to represent in the most favourable colours the world from which I came, I touched but slightly, though indulgently, on the antiquated and decaying institutions of Europe, in order to expatiate on the present grandeur and prospective pre-eminence of that glorious American Republic, in which Europe enviously seeks its model and tremblingly foresees its doom. Selecting for an example of the social life of the United States that city in which progress advances at the fastest rate, I indulged in an animated description of the moral habits of New York. Mortified to see, by the faces of my listeners, that I did not make the favourable impression I had anticipated, I elevated my theme; dwelling on the excellence of democratic institutions, their promotion of tranquil happiness by the government of party, and the mode in which they diffused such happiness throughout the community by preferring, for the exercise of power and the acquisition of honours, the lowliest citizens in point of property, education, and character. Fortunately recollecting the peroration of a speech, on the purifying influences of American democracy and their destined spread over the world, made by a certain eloquent senator (for whose vote in the Senate a Railway Company, to which my two brothers belonged, had just paid 20,000 dollars), I wound up by repeating its glowing predictions of the magnificent future that smiled upon mankind—when the flag of freedom should float over an entire continent, and two hundred millions of intelligent citizens, accustomed from infancy to the daily use of revolvers, should apply to a cowering universe the doctrine of the Patriot Monroe.

When I had concluded, my host gently shook his head, and fell into a musing study, making a sign to me and his daughter to remain silent while he reflected. And after a time he said, in a very earnest and solemn tone, "If you think as you say, that you, though a stranger, have received kindness at the hands of me and mine, I adjure you to reveal nothing to any other of our people respecting the world from which you came, unless, on consideration, I give you permission to do so. Do you consent to this request?" "Of course I pledge my word, to it," said I, somewhat amazed; and I extended my right hand to grasp his. But he placed my hand gently on his forehead and his own right hand on my breast, which is the custom amongst this race in all matters of promise or verbal obligations. Then turning to his daughter, he said, "And you, Zee, will not repeat to any one what the stranger has said, or may say, to me or to you, of a world other than our own." Zee rose and kissed her father on the temples, saying, with a smile, "A Gy's tongue is wanton, but love can fetter it fast. And if, my father, you fear lest a chance word from me or yourself could expose our community to danger, by a desire to explore a world beyond us, will not a wave of the 'vril,' properly impelled, wash even the memory of what we have heard the stranger say out of the tablets of the brain?"

"What is the vril?" I asked.

Therewith Zee began to enter into an explanation of which I understood very little, for there is no word in any language I know which is an exact synonym for vril. I should call it electricity, except that it comprehends in its manifold branches other forces of nature, to which, in our scientific nomenclature, differing names are assigned, such as magnetism, galvanism, &c. These people consider that in vril they have arrived at the unity in natural energetic agencies, which has been conjectured by many philosophers above ground, and which Faraday thus intimates under the more cautious term of correlation:—

"I have long held an opinion," says that illustrious experimentalist, "almost amounting to a conviction, in common, I believe, with many other lovers of natural knowledge, that the various forms under which the forces of matter are made manifest, have one common origin; or, in other words, are so directly related and mutually dependent that they are convertible, as it were into one another, and possess equivalents of power in their action."

These subterranean philosophers assert that by one operation of vril, which Faraday would perhaps call 'atmospheric magnetism,' they can influence the variations of temperature—in plain words, the weather; that by operations, akin to those ascribed to mesmerism, electro-biology, odic force, &c., but applied scientifically, through vril conductors, they can exercise influence over minds, and bodies animal and vegetable, to an extent not surpassed in the romances of our mystics. To all such agencies they give the common name of vril."

Zee asked me if, in my world, it was not known that all the faculties of the mind could be quickened to a degree unknown in the waking state, by trance or vision, in which the thoughts of one brain could be transmitted to another, and knowledge be thus rapidly interchanged. I replied, that there were amongst us stories told of such trance or vision, and that I had heard much and seen something in mesmeric clairvoyance; but that these practices had fallen much into disuse or contempt, partly because of the gross impostures to which they had been made subservient, and partly because, even where the effects upon certain abnormal constitutions were genuinely produced, the effects when fairly examined and analysed, were very unsatisfactory—not to be relied upon for any systematic truthfulness or any practical purpose, and rendered very mischievous to credulous persons by the superstitions they tended to produce. Zee received my answers with much benignant attention, and said that similar instances of abuse and credulity had been familiar to their own scientific experience in the infancy of their knowledge, and while the properties of vril were misapprehended, but that she reserved further discussion on this subject till I was more fitted to enter into it. She contented herself with adding, that it was through the agency of vril, while I had been placed in the state of trance, that I had been made acquainted with the rudiments of their language; and that she and her father, who alone of the family, took the pains to watch the experiment, had acquired a greater proportionate knowledge of my language than I of their own; partly because my language was much simpler than theirs, comprising far less of complex ideas; and partly because their organisation was, by hereditary culture, much more ductile and more readily capable of acquiring knowledge than mine. At this I secretly demurred; and having had in the course of a practical life, to sharpen my wits, whether at home or in travel, I could not allow that my cerebral organisation could possibly be duller than that of people who had lived all their lives by lamplight. However, while I was thus thinking, Zee quietly pointed her forefinger at my forehead, and sent me to sleep.

Chapter VIII.

When I once more awoke I saw by my bed-side the child who had brought the rope and grappling-hooks to the house in which I had been first received, and which, as I afterwards learned, was the residence of the chief magistrate of the tribe. The child, whose name was Taee (pronounced Tar-ee), was the magistrate's eldest son. I found that during my last sleep or trance I had made still greater advance in the language of the country, and could converse with comparative ease and fluency.

This child was singularly handsome, even for the beautiful race to which he belonged, with a countenance very manly in aspect for his years, and with a more vivacious and energetic expression than I had hitherto seen in the serene and passionless faces of the men. He brought me the tablet on which I had drawn the mode of my descent, and had also sketched the head of the horrible reptile that had scared me from my friend's corpse. Pointing to that part of the drawing, Taee put to me a few questions respecting the size and form of the monster, and the cave or chasm from which it had emerged. His interest in my answers seemed so grave as to divert him for a while from any curiosity as to myself or my antecedents. But to my great embarrassment, seeing how I was pledged to my host, he was just beginning to ask me where I came from, when Zee, fortunately entered, and, overhearing him, said, "Taee, give to our guest any information he may desire, but ask none from him in return. To question him who he is, whence he comes, or wherefore he is here, would be a breach of the law which my father has laid down in this house."

"So be it," said Taee, pressing his hand to his breast; and from that moment, till the one in which I saw him last, this child, with whom I became very intimate, never once put to me any of the questions thus interdicted.

Chapter IX.

It was not for some time, and until, by repeated trances, if they are to be so called, my mind became better prepared to interchange ideas with my entertainers, and more fully to comprehend differences of manners and customs, at first too strange to my experience to be seized by my reason, that I was enabled to gather the following details respecting the origin and history of the subterranean population, as portion of one great family race called the Ana.

According to the earliest traditions, the remote progenitors of the race had once tenanted a world above the surface of that in which their descendants dwelt. Myths of that world were still preserved in their archives, and in those myths were legends of a vaulted dome in which the lamps were lighted by no human hand. But such legends were considered by most commentators as allegorical fables. According to these traditions the earth itself, at the date to which the traditions ascend, was not indeed in its infancy, but in the throes and travail of transition from one form of development to another, and subject to many violent revolutions of nature. By one of such revolutions, that portion of the upper world inhabited by the ancestors of this race had been subjected to inundations, not rapid, but gradual and uncontrollable, in which all, save a scanty remnant, were submerged and perished. Whether this be a record of our historical and sacred Deluge, or of some earlier one contended for by geologists, I do not pretend to conjecture; though, according to the chronology of this people as compared with that of Newton, it must have been many thousands of years before the time of Noah. On the other hand, the account of these writers does not harmonise with the opinions most in vogue among geological authorities, inasmuch as it places the existence of a human race upon earth at dates long anterior to that assigned to the terrestrial formation adapted to the introduction of mammalia. A band of the ill-fated race, thus invaded by the Flood, had, during the march of the waters, taken refuge in caverns amidst the loftier rocks, and, wandering through these hollows, they lost sight of the upper world forever. Indeed, the whole face of the earth had been changed by this great revulsion; land had been turned into sea—sea into land. In the bowels of the inner earth, even now, I was informed as a positive fact, might be discovered the remains of human habitation—habitation not in huts and caverns, but in vast cities whose ruins attest the civilisation of races which flourished before the age of Noah, and are not to be classified with those genera to which philosophy ascribes the use of flint and the ignorance of iron.

The fugitives had carried with them the knowledge of the arts they had practised above ground—arts of culture and civilisation. Their earliest want must have been that of supplying below the earth the light they had lost above it; and at no time, even in the traditional period, do the races, of which the one I now sojourned with formed a tribe, seem to have been unacquainted with the art of extracting light from gases, or manganese, or petroleum. They had been accustomed in their former state to contend with the rude forces of nature; and indeed the lengthened battle they had fought with their conqueror Ocean, which had taken centuries in its spread, had quickened their skill in curbing waters into dikes and channels. To this skill they owed their preservation in their new abode. "For many generations," said my host, with a sort of contempt and horror, "these primitive forefathers are said to have degraded their rank and shortened their lives by eating the flesh of animals, many varieties of which had, like themselves, escaped the Deluge, and sought shelter in the hollows of the earth; other animals, supposed to be unknown to the upper world, those hollows themselves produced."

When what we should term the historical age emerged from the twilight of tradition, the Ana were already established in different communities, and had attained to a degree of civilisation very analogous to that which the more advanced nations above the earth now enjoy. They were familiar with most of our mechanical inventions, including the application of steam as well as gas. The communities were in fierce competition with each other. They had their rich and their poor; they had orators and conquerors; they made war either for a domain or an idea. Though the various states acknowledged various forms of government, free institutions were beginning to preponderate; popular assemblies increased in power; republics soon became general; the democracy to which the most enlightened European politicians look forward as the extreme goal of political advancement, and which still prevailed among other subterranean races, whom they despised as barbarians, the loftier family of Ana, to which belonged the tribe I was visiting, looked back to as one of the crude and ignorant experiments which belong to the infancy of political science. It was the age of envy and hate, of fierce passions, of constant social changes more or less violent, of strife between classes, of war between state and state. This phase of society lasted, however, for some ages, and was finally brought to a close, at least among the nobler and more intellectual populations, by the gradual discovery of the latent powers stored in the all-permeating fluid which they denominate Vril.

According to the account I received from Zee, who, as an erudite professor of the College of Sages, had studied such matters more diligently than any other member of my host's family, this fluid is capable of being raised and disciplined into the mightiest agency over all forms of matter, animate or inanimate. It can destroy like the flash of lightning; yet, differently applied, it can replenish or invigorate life, heal, and preserve, and on it they chiefly rely for the cure of disease, or rather for enabling the physical organisation to re-establish the due equilibrium of its natural powers, and thereby to cure itself. By this agency they rend way through the most solid substances, and open valleys for culture through the rocks of their subterranean wilderness. From it they extract the light which supplies their lamps, finding it steadier, softer, and healthier than the other inflammable materials they had formerly used.

But the effects of the alleged discovery of the means to direct the more terrible force of vril were chiefly remarkable in their influence upon social polity. As these effects became familiarly known and skillfully administered, war between the vril-discoverers ceased, for they brought the art of destruction to such perfection as to annul all superiority in numbers, discipline, or military skill. The fire lodged in the hollow of a rod directed by the hand of a child could shatter the strongest fortress, or cleave its burning way from the van to the rear of an embattled host. If army met army, and both had command of this agency, it could be but to the annihilation of each. The age of war was therefore gone, but with the cessation of war other effects bearing upon the social state soon became apparent. Man was so completely at the mercy of man, each whom he encountered being able, if so willing, to slay him on the instant, that all notions of government by force gradually vanished from political systems and forms of law. It is only by force that vast communities, dispersed through great distances of space, can be kept together; but now there was no longer either the necessity of self-preservation or the pride of aggrandisement to make one state desire to preponderate in population over another.

The Vril-discoverers thus, in the course of a few generations, peacefully split into communities of moderate size. The tribe amongst which I had fallen was limited to 12,000 families. Each tribe occupied a territory sufficient for all its wants, and at stated periods the surplus population departed to seek a realm of its own. There appeared no necessity for any arbitrary selection of these emigrants; there was always a sufficient number who volunteered to depart.

These subdivided states, petty if we regard either territory or population,—all appertained to one vast general family. They spoke the same language, though the dialects might slightly differ. They intermarried; They maintained the same general laws and customs; and so important a bond between these several communities was the knowledge of vril and the practice of its agencies, that the word A-Vril was synonymous with civilisation; and Vril-ya, signifying "The Civilised Nations," was the common name by which the communities employing the uses of vril distinguished themselves from such of the Ana as were yet in a state of barbarism.

The government of the tribe of Vril-ya I am treating of was apparently very complicated, really very simple. It was based upon a principle recognised in theory, though little carried out in practice, above ground—viz., that the object of all systems of philosophical thought tends to the attainment of unity, or the ascent through all intervening labyrinths to the simplicity of a single first cause or principle. Thus in politics, even republican writers have agreed that a benevolent autocracy would insure the best administration, if there were any guarantees for its continuance, or against its gradual abuse of the powers accorded to it. This singular community elected therefore a single supreme magistrate styled Tur; he held his office nominally for life, but he could seldom be induced to retain it after the first approach of old age. There was indeed in this society nothing to induce any of its members to covet the cares of office. No honours, no insignia of higher rank, were assigned to it. The supreme magistrate was not distinguished from the rest by superior habitation or revenue. On the other hand, the duties awarded to him were marvellously light and easy, requiring no preponderant degree of energy or intelligence. There being no apprehensions of war, there were no armies to maintain; there being no government of force, there was no police to appoint and direct. What we call crime was utterly unknown to the Vril-ya; and there were no courts of criminal justice. The rare instances of civil disputes were referred for arbitration to friends chosen by either party, or decided by the Council of Sages, which will be described later. There were no professional lawyers; and indeed their laws were but amicable conventions, for there was no power to enforce laws against an offender who carried in his staff the power to destroy his judges. There were customs and regulations to compliance with which, for several ages, the people had tacitly habituated themselves; or if in any instance an individual felt such compliance hard, he quitted the community and went elsewhere. There was, in fact, quietly established amid this state, much the same compact that is found in our private families, in which we virtually say to any independent grown-up member of the family whom we receive to entertain, "Stay or go, according as our habits and regulations suit or displease you." But though there were no laws such as we call laws, no race above ground is so law-observing. Obedience to the rule adopted by the community has become as much an instinct as if it were implanted by nature. Even in every household the head of it makes a regulation for its guidance, which is never resisted nor even cavilled at by those who belong to the family. They have a proverb, the pithiness of which is much lost in this paraphrase, "No happiness without order, no order without authority, no authority without unity." The mildness of all government among them, civil or domestic, may be signalised by their idiomatic expressions for such terms as illegal or forbidden— viz., "It is requested not to do so and so." Poverty among the Ana is as unknown as crime; not that property is held in common, or that all are equals in the extent of their possessions or the size and luxury of their habitations: but there being no difference of rank or position between the grades of wealth or the choice of occupations, each pursues his own inclinations without creating envy or vying; some like a modest, some a more splendid kind of life; each makes himself happy in his own way. Owing to this absence of competition, and the limit placed on the population, it is difficult for a family to fall into distress; there are no hazardous speculations, no emulators striving for superior wealth and rank. No doubt, in each settlement all originally had the same proportions of land dealt out to them; but some, more adventurous than others, had extended their possessions farther into the bordering wilds, or had improved into richer fertility the produce of their fields, or entered into commerce or trade. Thus, necessarily, some had grown richer than others, but none had become absolutely poor, or wanting anything which their tastes desired. If they did so, it was always in their power to migrate, or at the worst to apply, without shame and with certainty of aid, to the rich, for all the members of the community considered themselves as brothers of one affectionate and united family. More upon this head will be treated of incidentally as my narrative proceeds.

The chief care of the supreme magistrate was to communicate with certain active departments charged with the administration of special details. The most important and essential of such details was that connected with the due provision of light. Of this department my host, Aph-Lin, was the chief. Another department, which might be called the foreign, communicated with the neighbouring kindred states, principally for the purpose of ascertaining all new inventions; and to a third department all such inventions and improvements in machinery were committed for trial. Connected with this department was the College of Sages—a college especially favoured by such of the Ana as were widowed and childless, and by the young unmarried females, amongst whom Zee was the most active, and, if what we call renown or distinction was a thing acknowledged by this people (which I shall later show it is not), among the more renowned or distinguished. It is by the female Professors of this College that those studies which are deemed of least use in practical life—as purely speculative philosophy, the history of remote periods, and such sciences as entomology, conchology, &c.—are the more diligently cultivated. Zee, whose mind, active as Aristotle's, equally embraced the largest domains and the minutest details of thought, had written two volumes on the parasite insect that dwells amid the hairs of a tiger's* paw, which work was considered the best authority on that interesting subject.

* The animal here referred to has many points of difference from the tiger of the upper world. It is larger, and with a broader paw, and still more receding frontal. It haunts the side of lakes and pools, and feeds principally on fishes, though it does not object to any terrestrial animal of inferior strength that comes in its way. It is becoming very scarce even in the wild districts, where it is devoured by gigantic reptiles. I apprehended that it clearly belongs to the tiger species, since the parasite animalcule found in its paw, like that in the Asiatic tiger, is a miniature image of itself.

But the researches of the sages are not confined to such subtle or elegant studies. They comprise various others more important, and especially the properties of vril, to the perception of which their finer nervous organisation renders the female Professors eminently keen. It is out of this college that the Tur, or chief magistrate, selects Councillors, limited to three, in the rare instances in which novelty of event or circumstance perplexes his own judgment.

There are a few other departments of minor consequence, but all are carried on so noiselessly, and quietly that the evidence of a government seems to vanish altogether, and social order to be as regular and unobtrusive as if it were a law of nature. Machinery is employed to an inconceivable extent in all the operations of labour within and without doors, and it is the unceasing object of the department charged with its administration to extend its efficiency. There is no class of labourers or servants, but all who are required to assist or control the machinery are found in the children, from the time they leave the care of their mothers to the marriageable age, which they place at sixteen for the Gy-ei (the females), twenty for the Ana (the males). These children are formed into bands and sections under their own chiefs, each following the pursuits in which he is most pleased, or for which he feels himself most fitted. Some take to handicrafts, some to agriculture, some to household work, and some to the only services of danger to which the population is exposed; for the sole perils that threaten this tribe are, first, from those occasional convulsions within the earth, to foresee and guard against which tasks their utmost ingenuity—irruptions of fire and water, the storms of subterranean winds and escaping gases. At the borders of the domain, and at all places where such peril might be apprehended, vigilant inspectors are stationed with telegraphic communications to the hall in which chosen sages take it by turns to hold perpetual sittings. These inspectors are always selected from the elder boys approaching the age of puberty, and on the principle that at that age observation is more acute and the physical forces more alert than at any other. The second service of danger, less grave, is in the destruction of all creatures hostile to the life, or the culture, or even the comfort, of the Ana. Of these the most formidable are the vast reptiles, of some of which antediluvian relics are preserved in our museums, and certain gigantic winged creatures, half bird, half reptile. These, together with lesser wild animals, corresponding to our tigers or venomous serpents, it is left to the younger children to hunt and destroy; because, according to the Ana, here ruthlessness is wanted, and the younger the child the more ruthlessly he will destroy. There is another class of animals in the destruction of which discrimination is to be used, and against which children of intermediate age are appointed—animals that do not threaten the life of man, but ravage the produce of his labour, varieties of the elk and deer species, and a smaller creature much akin to our rabbit, though infinitely more destructive to crops, and much more cunning in its mode of depredation. It is the first object of these appointed infants, to tame the more intelligent of such animals into respect for enclosures signalised by conspicuous landmarks, as dogs are taught to respect a larder, or even to guard the master's property. It is only where such creatures are found untamable to this extent that they are destroyed. Life is never taken away for food or for sport, and never spared where untamably inimical to the Ana. Concomitantly with these bodily services and tasks, the mental education of the children goes on till boyhood ceases. It is the general custom, then, to pass though a course of instruction at the College of Sages, in which, besides more general studies, the pupil receives special lessons in such vocation or direction of intellect as he himself selects. Some, however, prefer to pass this period of probation in travel, or to emigrate, or to settle down at once into rural or commercial pursuits. No force is put upon individual inclination.

Chapter X.

The word Ana (pronounced broadly 'Arna') corresponds with our plural 'men;' An (pronounced 'Arn'), the singular, with 'man.' The word for woman is Gy (pronounced hard, as in Guy); it forms itself into Gy-ei for the plural, but the G becomes soft in the plural like Jy-ei. They have a proverb to the effect that this difference in pronunciation is symbolical, for that the female sex is soft in the concrete, but hard to deal with in the individual. The Gy-ei are in the fullest enjoyment of all the rights of equality with males, for which certain philosophers above ground contend.

In childhood they perform the offices of work and labour impartially with the boys, and, indeed, in the earlier age appropriated to the destruction of animals irreclaimably hostile, the girls are frequently preferred, as being by constitution more ruthless under the influence of fear or hate. In the interval between infancy and the marriageable age familiar intercourse between the sexes is suspended. At the marriageable age it is renewed, never with worse consequences than those which attend upon marriage. All arts and vocations allotted to the one sex are open to the other, and the Gy-ei arrogate to themselves a superiority in all those abstruse and mystical branches of reasoning, for which they say the Ana are unfitted by a duller sobriety of understanding, or the routine of their matter-of-fact occupations, just as young ladies in our own world constitute themselves authorities in the subtlest points of theological doctrine, for which few men, actively engaged in worldly business have sufficient learning or refinement of intellect. Whether owing to early training in gymnastic exercises, or to their constitutional organisation, the Gy-ei are usually superior to the Ana in physical strength (an important element in the consideration and maintenance of female rights). They attain to loftier stature, and amid their rounder proportions are imbedded sinews and muscles as hardy as those of the other sex. Indeed they assert that, according to the original laws of nature, females were intended to be larger than males, and maintain this dogma by reference to the earliest formations of life in insects, and in the most ancient family of the vertebrata—viz., fishes—in both of which the females are generally large enough to make a meal of their consorts if they so desire. Above all, the Gy-ei have a readier and more concentred power over that mysterious fluid or agency which contains the element of destruction, with a larger portion of that sagacity which comprehends dissimulation. Thus they cannot only defend themselves against all aggressions from the males, but could, at any moment when he least expected his danger, terminate the existence of an offending spouse. To the credit of the Gy-ei no instance of their abuse of this awful superiority in the art of destruction is on record for several ages. The last that occurred in the community I speak of appears (according to their chronology) to have been about two thousand years ago. A Gy, then, in a fit of jealousy, slew her husband; and this abominable act inspired such terror among the males that they emigrated in a body and left all the Gy-ei to themselves. The history runs that the widowed Gy-ei, thus reduced to despair, fell upon the murderess when in her sleep (and therefore unarmed), and killed her, and then entered into a solemn obligation amongst themselves to abrogate forever the exercise of their extreme conjugal powers, and to inculcate the same obligation for ever and ever on their female children. By this conciliatory process, a deputation despatched to the fugitive consorts succeeded in persuading many to return, but those who did return were mostly the elder ones. The younger, either from too craven a doubt of their consorts, or too high an estimate of their own merits, rejected all overtures, and, remaining in other communities, were caught up there by other mates, with whom perhaps they were no better off. But the loss of so large a portion of the male youth operated as a salutary warning on the Gy-ei, and confirmed them in the pious resolution to which they pledged themselves. Indeed it is now popularly considered that, by long hereditary disuse, the Gy-ei have lost both the aggressive and defensive superiority over the Ana which they once possessed, just as in the inferior animals above the earth many peculiarities in their original formation, intended by nature for their protection, gradually fade or become inoperative when not needed under altered circumstances. I should be sorry, however, for any An who induced a Gy to make the experiment whether he or she were the stronger.

From the incident I have narrated, the Ana date certain alterations in the marriage customs, tending, perhaps, somewhat to the advantage of the male. They now bind themselves in wedlock only for three years; at the end of each third year either male or female can divorce the other and is free to marry again. At the end of ten years the An has the privilege of taking a second wife, allowing the first to retire if she so please. These regulations are for the most part a dead letter; divorces and polygamy are extremely rare, and the marriage state now seems singularly happy and serene among this astonishing people;—the Gy-ei, notwithstanding their boastful superiority in physical strength and intellectual abilities, being much curbed into gentle manners by the dread of separation or of a second wife, and the Ana being very much the creatures of custom, and not, except under great aggravation, likely to exchange for hazardous novelties faces and manners to which they are reconciled by habit. But there is one privilege the Gy-ei carefully retain, and the desire for which perhaps forms the secret motive of most lady asserters of woman rights above ground. They claim the privilege, here usurped by men, of proclaiming their love and urging their suit; in other words, of being the wooing party rather than the wooed. Such a phenomenon as an old maid does not exist among the Gy-ei. Indeed it is very seldom that a Gy does not secure any An upon whom she sets her heart, if his affections be not strongly engaged elsewhere. However coy, reluctant, and prudish, the male she courts may prove at first, yet her perseverance, her ardour, her persuasive powers, her command over the mystic agencies of vril, are pretty sure to run down his neck into what we call "the fatal noose." Their argument for the reversal of that relationship of the sexes which the blind tyranny of man has established on the surface of the earth, appears cogent, and is advanced with a frankness which might well be commended to impartial consideration. They say, that of the two the female is by nature of a more loving disposition than the male—that love occupies a larger space in her thoughts, and is more essential to her happiness, and that therefore she ought to be the wooing party; that otherwise the male is a shy and dubitant creature—that he has often a selfish predilection for the single state—that he often pretends to misunderstand tender glances and delicate hints—that, in short, he must be resolutely pursued and captured. They add, moreover, that unless the Gy can secure the An of her choice, and one whom she would not select out of the whole world becomes her mate, she is not only less happy than she otherwise would be, but she is not so good a being, that her qualities of heart are not sufficiently developed; whereas the An is a creature that less lastingly concentrates his affections on one object; that if he cannot get the Gy whom he prefers he easily reconciles himself to another Gy; and, finally, that at the worst, if he is loved and taken care of, it is less necessary to the welfare of his existence that he should love as well as be loved; he grows contented with his creature comforts, and the many occupations of thought which he creates for himself.

Whatever may be said as to this reasoning, the system works well for the male; for being thus sure that he is truly and ardently loved, and that the more coy and reluctant he shows himself, the more determination to secure him increases, he generally contrives to make his consent dependent on such conditions as he thinks the best calculated to insure, if not a blissful, at least a peaceful life. Each individual An has his own hobbies, his own ways, his own predilections, and, whatever they may be, he demands a promise of full and unrestrained concession to them. This, in the pursuit of her object, the Gy readily promises; and as the characteristic of this extraordinary people is an implicit veneration for truth, and her word once given is never broken even by the giddiest Gy, the conditions stipulated for are religiously observed. In fact, notwithstanding all their abstract rights and powers, the Gy-ei are the most amiable, conciliatory, and submissive wives I have ever seen even in the happiest households above ground. It is an aphorism among them, that "where a Gy loves it is her pleasure to obey." It will be observed that in the relationship of the sexes I have spoken only of marriage, for such is the moral perfection to which this community has attained, that any illicit connection is as little possible amongst them as it would be to a couple of linnets during the time they agree to live in pairs.

Chapter XI.

Nothing had more perplexed me in seeking to reconcile my sense to the existence of regions extending below the surface of the earth, and habitable by beings, if dissimilar from, still, in all material points of organism, akin to those in the upper world, than the contradiction thus presented to the doctrine in which, I believe, most geologists and philosophers concur—viz., that though with us the sun is the great source of heat, yet the deeper we go beneath the crust of the earth, the greater is the increasing heat, being, it is said, found in the ratio of a degree for every foot, commencing from fifty feet below the surface. But though the domains of the tribe I speak of were, on the higher ground, so comparatively near to the surface, that I could account for a temperature, therein, suitable to organic life, yet even the ravines and valleys of that realm were much less hot than philosophers would deem possible at such a depth—certainly not warmer than the south of France, or at least of Italy. And according to all the accounts I received, vast tracts immeasurably deeper beneath the surface, and in which one might have thought only salamanders could exist, were inhabited by innumerable races organised like ourselves, I cannot pretend in any way to account for a fact which is so at variance with the recognised laws of science, nor could Zee much help me towards a solution of it. She did but conjecture that sufficient allowance had not been made by our philosophers for the extreme porousness of the interior earth—the vastness of its cavities and irregularities, which served to create free currents of air and frequent winds—and for the various modes in which heat is evaporated and thrown off. She allowed, however, that there was a depth at which the heat was deemed to be intolerable to such organised life as was known to the experience of the Vril-ya, though their philosophers believed that even in such places life of some kind, life sentient, life intellectual, would be found abundant and thriving, could the philosophers penetrate to it. "Wherever the All-Good builds," said she, "there, be sure, He places inhabitants. He loves not empty dwellings." She added, however, that many changes in temperature and climate had been effected by the skill of the Vril-ya, and that the agency of vril had been successfully employed in such changes. She described a subtle and life-giving medium called Lai, which I suspect to be identical with the ethereal oxygen of Dr. Lewins, wherein work all the correlative forces united under the name of vril; and contended that wherever this medium could be expanded, as it were, sufficiently for the various agencies of vril to have ample play, a temperature congenial to the highest forms of life could be secured. She said also, that it was the belief of their naturalists that flowers and vegetation had been produced originally (whether developed from seeds borne from the surface of the earth in the earlier convulsions of nature, or imported by the tribes that first sought refuge in cavernous hollows) through the operations of the light constantly brought to bear on them, and the gradual improvement in culture. She said also, that since the vril light had superseded all other light-giving bodies, the colours of flower and foliage had become more brilliant, and vegetation had acquired larger growth.

Leaving these matters to the consideration of those better competent to deal with them, I must now devote a few pages to the very interesting questions connected with the language of the Vril-ya.

Chapter XII.

The language of the Vril-ya is peculiarly interesting, because it seems to me to exhibit with great clearness the traces of the three main transitions through which language passes in attaining to perfection of form.

One of the most illustrious of recent philologists, Max Muller, in arguing for the analogy between the strata of language and the strata of the earth, lays down this absolute dogma: "No language can, by any possibility, be inflectional without having passed through the agglutinative and isolating stratum. No language can be agglutinative without clinging with its roots to the underlying stratum of isolation."—'On the Stratification of Language,' p. 20.

Taking then the Chinese language as the best existing type of the original isolating stratum, "as the faithful photograph of man in his leading-strings trying the muscles of his mind, groping his way, and so delighted with his first successful grasps that he repeats them again and again," (Max Muller, p. 3)—we have, in the language of the Vril-ya, still "clinging with its roots to the underlying stratum," the evidences of the original isolation. It abounds in monosyllables, which are the foundations of the language. The transition into the agglutinative form marks an epoch that must have gradually extended through ages, the written literature of which has only survived in a few fragments of symbolical mythology and certain pithy sentences which have passed into popular proverbs. With the extant literature of the Vril-ya the inflectional stratum commences. No doubt at that time there must have operated concurrent causes, in the fusion of races by some dominant people, and the rise of some great literary phenomena by which the form of language became arrested and fixed. As the inflectional stage prevailed over the agglutinative, it is surprising to see how much more boldly the original roots of the language project from the surface that conceals them. In the old fragments and proverbs of the preceding stage the monosyllables which compose those roots vanish amidst words of enormous length, comprehending whole sentences from which no one part can be disentangled from the other and employed separately. But when the inflectional form of language became so far advanced as to have its scholars and grammarians, they seem to have united in extirpating all such polysynthetical or polysyllabic monsters, as devouring invaders of the aboriginal forms. Words beyond three syllables became proscribed as barbarous and in proportion as the language grew thus simplified it increased in strength, in dignity, and in sweetness. Though now very compressed in sound, it gains in clearness by that compression. By a single letter, according to its position, they contrive to express all that with civilised nations in our upper world it takes the waste, sometimes of syllables, sometimes of sentences, to express. Let me here cite one or two instances: An (which I will translate man), Ana (men); the letter 's' is with them a letter implying multitude, according to where it is placed; Sana means mankind; Ansa, a multitude of men. The prefix of certain letters in their alphabet invariably denotes compound significations. For instance, Gl (which with them is a single letter, as 'th' is a single letter with the Greeks) at the commencement of a word infers an assemblage or union of things, sometimes kindred, sometimes dissimilar—as Oon, a house; Gloon, a town (i. e., an assemblage of houses). Ata is sorrow; Glata, a public calamity. Aur-an is the health or wellbeing of a man; Glauran, the wellbeing of the state, the good of the community; and a word constantly in ther mouths is A-glauran, which denotes their political creed—viz., that "the first principle of a community is the good of all." Aub is invention; Sila, a tone in music. Glaubsila, as uniting the ideas of invention and of musical intonation, is the classical word for poetry—abbreviated, in ordinary conversation, to Glaubs. Na, which with them is, like Gl, but a single letter, always, when an initial, implies something antagonistic to life or joy or comfort, resembling in this the Aryan root Nak, expressive of perishing or destruction. Nax is darkness; Narl, death; Naria, sin or evil. Nas—an uttermost condition of sin and evil—corruption. In writing, they deem it irreverent to express the Supreme Being by any special name. He is symbolized by what may be termed the heiroglyphic of a pyramid, /\. In prayer they address Him by a name which they deem too sacred to confide to a stranger, and I know it not. In conversation they generally use a periphrastic epithet, such as the All-Good. The letter V, symbolical of the inverted pyramid, where it is an initial, nearly always denotes excellence of power; as Vril, of which I have said so much; Veed, an immortal spirit; Veed-ya, immortality; Koom, pronounced like the Welsh Cwm, denotes something of hollowness. Koom itself is a cave; Koom-in, a hole; Zi-koom, a valley; Koom-zi, vacancy or void; Bodh-koom, ignorance (literally, knowledge-void). Koom-posh is their name for the government of the many, or the ascendancy of the most ignorant or hollow. Posh is an almost untranslatable idiom, implying, as the reader will see later, contempt. The closest rendering I can give to it is our slang term, "bosh;" and this Koom-Posh may be loosely rendered "Hollow-Bosh." But when Democracy or Koom-Posh degenerates from popular ignorance into that popular passion or ferocity which precedes its decease, as (to cite illustrations from the upper world) during the French Reign of Terror, or for the fifty years of the Roman Republic preceding the ascendancy of Augustus, their name for that state of things is Glek-Nas. Ek is strife—Glek, the universal strife. Nas, as I before said, is corruption or rot; thus, Glek-Nas may be construed, "the universal strife-rot." Their compounds are very expressive; thus, Bodh being knowledge, and Too a participle that implies the action of cautiously approaching,—Too-bodh is their word for Philosophy; Pah is a contemptuous exclamation analogous to our idiom, "stuff and nonsense;" Pah-bodh (literally stuff and nonsense-knowledge) is their term for futile and false philosophy, and applied to a species of metaphysical or speculative ratiocination formerly in vogue, which consisted in making inquiries that could not be answered, and were not worth making; such, for instance, as "Why does an An have five toes to his feet instead of four or six? Did the first An, created by the All-Good, have the same number of toes as his descendants? In the form by which an An will be recognised by his friends in the future state of being, will he retain any toes at all, and, if so, will they be material toes or spiritual toes?" I take these illustrations of Pahbodh, not in irony or jest, but because the very inquiries I name formed the subject of controversy by the latest cultivators of that 'science,'—4000 years ago.

In the declension of nouns I was informed that anciently there were eight cases (one more than in the Sanskrit Grammar); but the effect of time has been to reduce these cases, and multiply, instead of these varying terminations, explanatory propositions. At present, in the Grammar submitted to my study, there were four cases to nouns, three having varying terminations, and the fourth a differing prefix.

SINGULAR.		PLURAL.	
Nom.	An, Man,	Nom.	Ana, Men.
Dat.	Ano, to Man,	Dat.	Anoi, to Men.
Ac.	Anan, Man,	Ac.	Ananda, Men.
Voc.	Hil-an, O Man,	Voc.	Hil-Ananda, O Men.

In the elder inflectional literature the dual form existed—it has long been obsolete.

The genitive case with them is also obsolete; the dative supplies its place: they say the House 'to' a Man, instead of the House 'of' a Man. When used (sometimes in poetry), the genitive in the termination is the same as the nominative; so is the ablative, the preposition that marks it being a prefix or suffix at option, and generally decided by ear, according to the sound of the noun. It will be observed that the prefix Hil marks the vocative case. It is always retained in addressing another, except in the most intimate domestic relations; its omission would be considered rude: just as in our of forms of speech in addressing a king it would have been deemed disrespectful to say "King," and reverential to say "O King." In fact, as they have no titles of honour, the vocative adjuration supplies the place of a title, and is given impartially to all. The prefix Hil enters into the composition of words that imply distant communications, as Hil-ya, to travel.

In the conjugation of their verbs, which is much too lengthy a subject to enter on here, the auxiliary verb Ya, "to go," which plays so considerable part in the Sanskrit, appears and performs a kindred office, as if it were a radical in some language from which both had descended. But another auxiliary or opposite signification also accompanies it and shares its labours—viz., Zi, to stay or repose. Thus Ya enters into the future tense, and Zi in the preterite of all verbs requiring auxiliaries. Yam, I shall go—Yiam, I may go—Yani-ya, I shall go (literally, I go to go), Zam-poo-yan, I have gone (literally, I rest from gone). Ya, as a termination, implies by analogy, progress, movement, efflorescence. Zi, as a terminal, denotes fixity, sometimes in a good sense, sometimes in a bad, according to the word with which it is coupled. Iva-zi, eternal goodness; Nan-zi, eternal evil. Poo (from) enters as a prefix to words that denote repugnance, or things from which we ought to be averse. Poo-pra, disgust; Poo-naria, falsehood, the vilest kind of evil. Poosh or Posh I have already confessed to be untranslatable literally. It is an expression of contempt not unmixed with pity. This radical seems to have originated from inherent sympathy between the labial effort and the sentiment that impelled it, Poo being an utterance in which the breath is exploded from the lips with more or less vehemence. On the other hand, Z, when an initial, is with them a sound in which the breath is sucked inward, and thus Zu, pronounced Zoo (which in their language is one letter), is the ordinary prefix to words that signify something that attracts, pleases, touches the heart—as Zummer, lover; Zutze, love; Zuzulia, delight. This indrawn sound of Z seems indeed naturally appropriate to fondness. Thus, even in our language, mothers say to their babies, in defiance of grammar, "Zoo darling;" and I have heard a learned professor at Boston call his wife (he had been only married a month) "Zoo little pet."

I cannot quit this subject, however, without observing by what slight changes in the dialects favoured by different tribes of the same race, the original signification and beauty of sounds may become confused and deformed. Zee told me with much indignation that Zummer (lover) which in the way she uttered it, seemed slowly taken down to the very depths of her heart, was, in some not very distant communities of the Vril-ya, vitiated into the half-hissing, half-nasal, wholly disagreeable, sound of Subber. I thought to myself it only wanted the introduction of 'n' before 'u' to render it into an English word significant of the last quality an amorous Gy would desire in her Zummer.

I will but mention another peculiarity in this language which gives equal force and brevity to its forms of expressions.

A is with them, as with us, the first letter of the alphabet, and is often used as a prefix word by itself to convey a complex idea of sovereignty or chiefdom, or presiding principle. For instance, Iva is goodness; Diva, goodness and happiness united; A-Diva is unerring and absolute truth. I have already noticed the value of A in A-glauran, so, in vril (to whose properties they trace their present state of civilisation), A-vril, denotes, as I have said, civilisation itself.

The philologist will have seen from the above how much the language of the Vril-ya is akin to the Aryan or Indo-Germanic; but, like all languages, it contains words and forms in which transfers from very opposite sources of speech have been taken. The very title of Tur, which they give to their supreme magistrate, indicates theft from a tongue akin to the Turanian. They say themselves that this is a foreign word borrowed from a title which their historical records show to have been borne by the chief of a nation with whom the ancestors of the Vril-ya were, in very remote periods, on friendly terms, but which has long become extinct, and they say that when, after the discovery of vril, they remodelled their political institutions, they expressly adopted a title taken from an extinct race and a dead language for that of their chief magistrate, in order to avoid all titles for that office with which they had previous associations.

Should life be spared to me, I may collect into systematic form such knowledge as I acquired of this language during my sojourn amongst the Vril-ya. But what I have already said will perhaps suffice to show to genuine philological students that a language which, preserving so many of the roots in the aboriginal form, and clearing from the immediate, but transitory, polysynthetical stage so many rude incumbrances, has attained to such a union of simplicity and compass in its final inflectional forms, must have been the gradual work of countless ages and many varieties of mind ; that it contains the evidence of fusion between congenial races, and necessitated, in arriving at the shape of which I have given examples, the continuous culture of a highly thoughtful people.

That, nevertheless, the literature which belongs to this language is a literature of the past; that the present felicitous state of society at which the Ana have attained forbids the progressive cultivation of literature, especially in the two main divisions of fiction and history, —I shall have occasion to show.

Chapter XIII.

This people have a religion, and, whatever may be said against it, at least it has these strange peculiarities: firstly, that all believe in the creed they profess; secondly, that they all practice the precepts which the creed inculcates. They unite in the worship of one divine Creator and Sustainer of the universe. They believe that it is one of the properties of the all-permeating agency of vril, to transmit to the well-spring of life and intelligence every thought that a living creature can conceive; and though they do not contend that the idea of a Diety is innate, yet they say that the An (man) is the only creature, so far as their observation of nature extends, to whom 'the capacity of conceiving that idea,' with all the trains of thought which open out from it, is vouchsafed. They hold that this capacity is a privilege that cannot have been given in vain, and hence that prayer and thanksgiving are acceptable to the divine Creator, and necessary to the complete development of the human creature. They offer their devotions both in private and public. Not being considered one of their species, I was not admitted into the building or temple in which the public worship is rendered; but I am informed that the service is exceedingly short, and unattended with any pomp of ceremony. It is a doctrine with the Vril-ya, that earnest devotion or complete abstraction from the actual world cannot, with benefit to itself, be maintained long at a stretch by the human mind, especially in public, and that all attempts to do so either lead to fanaticism or to hypocrisy. When they pray in private, it is when they are alone or with their young children.

They say that in ancient times there was a great number of books written upon speculations as to the nature of the Diety, and upon the forms of belief or worship supposed to be most agreeable to Him. But these were found to lead to such heated and angry disputations as not only to shake the peace of the community and divide families before the most united, but in the course of discussing the attributes of the Diety, the existence of the Diety Himself became argued away, or, what was worse, became invested with the passions and infirmities of the human disputants. "For," said my host, "since a finite being like an An cannot possibly define the Infinite, so, when he endeavours to realise an idea of the Divinity, he only reduces the Divinity into an An like himself." During the later ages, therefore, all theological speculations, though not forbidden, have been so discouraged as to have fallen utterly into disuse. The Vril-ya unite in a conviction of a future state, more felicitous and more perfect than the present. If they have very vague notions of the doctrine of rewards and punishments, it is perhaps because they have no systems of rewards and punishments among themselves, for there are no crimes to punish, and their moral standard is so even that no An among them is, upon the whole, considered more virtuous than another. If one excels, perhaps in one virtue, another equally excels in some other virtue; If one has his prevalent fault or infirmity, so also another has his. In fact, in their extraordinary mode of life. There are so few temptations to wrong, that they are good (according to their notions of goodness) merely because they live. They have some fanciful notions upon the continuance of life, when once bestowed, even in the vegetable world, as the reader will see in the next chapter.

Chapter XIV.

Though, as I have said, the Vril-ya discourage all speculations on the nature of the Supreme Being, they appear to concur in a belief by which they think to solve that great problem of the existence of evil which has so perplexed the philosophy of the upper world. They hold that wherever He has once given life, with the perceptions of that life, however faint it be, as in a plant, the life is never destroyed; it passes into new and improved forms, though not in this planet (differing therein from the ordinary doctrine of metempsychosis), and that the living thing retains the sense of identity, so that it connects its past life with its future, and is 'conscious' of its progressive improvement in the scale of joy. For they say that, without this assumption, they cannot, according to the lights of human reason vouchsafed to them, discover the perfect justice which must be a constituent quality of the All-Wise and the All-Good. Injustice, they say, can only emanate from three causes: want of wisdom to perceive what is just, want of benevolence to desire, want of power to fulfill it; and that each of these three wants is incompatible in the All-Wise, the All-Good, the All-Powerful. But that, while even in this life, the wisdom, the benevolence, and the power of the Supreme Being are sufficiently apparent to compel our recognition, the justice necessarily resulting from those attributes, absolutely requires another life, not for man only, but for every living thing of the inferior orders. That, alike in the animal and the vegetable world, we see one individual rendered, by circumstances beyond its control, exceedingly wretched compared to its neighbours—one only exists as the prey of another—even a plant suffers from disease till it perishes prematurely, while the plant next to it rejoices in its vitality and lives out its happy life free from a pang. That it is an erroneous analogy from human infirmities to reply by saying that the Supreme Being only acts by general laws, thereby making his own secondary causes so potent as to mar the essential kindness of the First Cause; and a still meaner and more ignorant conception of the All-Good, to dismiss with a brief contempt all consideration of justice for the myriad forms into which He has infused life, and assume that justice is only due to the single product of the An. There is no small and no great in the eyes of the divine Life-Giver. But once grant that nothing, however humble, which feels that it lives and suffers, can perish through the series of ages, that all its suffering here, if continuous from the moment of its birth to that of its transfer to another form of being, would be more brief compared with eternity than the cry of the new-born is compared to the whole life of a man; and once suppose that this living thing retains its sense of identity when so transformed (for without that sense it could be aware of no future being), and though, indeed, the fulfilment of divine justice is removed from the scope of our ken, yet we have a right to assume it to be uniform and universal, and not varying and partial, as it would be if acting only upon general and secondary laws; because such perfect justice flows of necessity from perfectness of knowledge to conceive, perfectness of love to will, and perfectness of power to complete it.

However fantastic this belief of the Vril-ya may be, it tends perhaps to confirm politically the systems of government which, admitting different degrees of wealth, yet establishes perfect equality in rank, exquisite mildness in all relations and intercourse, and tenderness to all created things which the good of the community does not require them to destroy. And though their notion of compensation to a tortured insect or a cankered flower may seem to some of us a very wild crotchet, yet, at least, is not a mischievous one; and it may furnish matter for no unpleasing reflection to think that within the abysses of earth, never lit by a ray from the material heavens, there should have penetrated so luminous a conviction of the ineffable goodness of the Creator—so fixed an idea that the general laws by which He acts cannot admit of any partial injustice or evil, and therefore cannot be comprehended without reference to their action over all space and throughout all time. And since, as I shall have occasion to observe later, the intellectual conditions and social systems of this subterranean race comprise and harmonise great, and apparently antagonistic, varieties in philosophical doctrine and speculation which have from time to time been started, discussed, dismissed, and have re-appeared amongst thinkers or dreamers in the upper world,—so I may perhaps appropriately conclude this reference to the belief of the Vril-ya, that self-conscious or sentient life once given is indestructible among inferior creatures as well as in man, by an eloquent passage from the work of that eminent zoologist, Louis Agassiz, which I have only just met with, many years after I had committed to paper these recollections of the life of the Vril-ya which I now reduce into something like arrangement and form: "The relations which individual animals bear to one another are of such a character that they ought long ago to have been considered as sufficient proof that no organised being could ever have been called into existence by other agency than by the direct intervention of a reflective mind. This argues strongly in favour of the existence in every animal of an immaterial principle similar to that which by its excellence and superior endowments places man so much above the animals; yet the principle unquestionably exists, and whether it be called sense, reason, or instinct, it presents in the whole range of organised beings a series of phenomena closely linked together, and upon it are based not only the higher manifestations of the mind, but the very permanence of the specific differences which characterise every organism. Most of the arguments in favour of the immortality of man apply equally to the permanency of this principle in other living beings. May I not add that a future life in which man would be deprived of that great source of enjoyment and intellectual and moral improvement which results from the contemplation of the harmonies of an organic world would involve a lamentable loss? And may we not look to a spiritual concert of the combined worlds and ALL their inhabitants in the presence of their Creator as the highest conception of paradise?"—'Essay on Classification,' sect. xvii. p. 97-99.

Chapter XV.

Kind to me as I found all in this household, the young daughter of my host was the most considerate and thoughtful in her kindness. At her suggestion I laid aside the habiliments in which I had descended from the upper earth, and adopted the dress of the Vril-ya, with the exception of the artful wings which served them, when on foot, as a graceful mantle. But as many of the Vril-ya, when occupied in urban pursuits, did not wear these wings, this exception created no marked difference between myself and the race among whom I sojourned, and I was thus enabled to visit the town without exciting unpleasant curiosity. Out of the household no one suspected that I had come from the upper world, and I was but regarded as one of some inferior and barbarous tribe whom Aph-Lin entertained as a guest.

The city was large in proportion to the territory round it, which was of no greater extent than many an English or Hungarian nobleman's estate; but the whole if it, to the verge of the rocks which constituted its boundary, was cultivated to the nicest degree, except where certain allotments of mountain and pasture were humanely left free to the sustenance of the harmless animals they had tamed, though not for domestic use. So great is their kindness towards these humbler creatures, that a sum is devoted from the public treasury for the purpose of deporting them to other Vril-ya communities willing to receive them (chiefly new colonies), whenever they become too numerous for the pastures allotted to them in their native place. They do not, however, multiply to an extent comparable to the ratio at which, with us, animals bred for slaughter, increase. It seems a law of nature that animals not useful to man gradually recede from the domains he occupies, or even become extinct. It is an old custom of the various sovereign states amidst which the race of the Vril-ya are distributed, to leave between each state a neutral and uncultivated border-land. In the instance of the community I speak of, this tract, being a ridge of savage rocks, was impassable by foot, but was easily surmounted, whether by the wings of the inhabitants or the air-boats, of which I shall speak hereafter. Roads through it were also cut for the transit of vehicles impelled by vril. These intercommunicating tracts were always kept lighted, and the expense thereof defrayed by a special tax, to which all the communities comprehended in the denomination of Vril-ya contribute in settled proportions. By these means a considerable commercial traffic with other states, both near and distant, was carried on. The surplus wealth on this special community was chiefly agricultural. The community was also eminent for skill in constructing implements connected with the arts of husbandry. In exchange for such merchandise it obtained articles more of luxury than necessity. There were few things imported on which they set a higher price than birds taught to pipe artful tunes in concert. These were brought from a great distance, and were marvellous for beauty of song and plumage. I understand that extraordinary care was taken by their breeders and teachers in selection, and that the species had wonderfully improved during the last few years. I saw no other pet animals among this community except some very amusing and sportive creatures of the Batrachian species, resembling frogs, but with very intelligent countenances, which the children were fond of, and kept in their private gardens. They appear to have no animals akin to our dogs or horses, though that learned naturalist, Zee, informed me that such creatures had once existed in those parts, and might now be found in regions inhabited by other races than the Vril-ya. She said that they had gradually disappeared from the more civilised world since the discovery of vril, and the results attending that discovery had dispensed with their uses. Machinery and the invention of wings had superseded the horse as a beast of burden; and the dog was no longer wanted either for protection or the chase, as it had been when the ancestors of the Vril-ya feared the aggressions of their own kind, or hunted the lesser animals for food. Indeed, however, so far as the horse was concerned, this region was so rocky that a horse could have been, there, of little use either for pastime or burden. The only creature they use for the latter purpose is a kind of large goat which is much employed on farms. The nature of the surrounding soil in these districts may be said to have first suggested the invention of wings and air-boats. The largeness of space in proportion to the space occupied by the city, was occasioned by the custom of surrounding every house with a separate garden. The broad main street, in which Aph-Lin dwelt, expanded into a vast square, in which were placed the College of Sages and all the public offices; a magnificent fountain of the luminous fluid which I call naptha (I am ignorant of its real nature) in the centre. All these public edifices have a uniform character of massiveness and solidity. They reminded me of the architectural pictures of Martin. Along the upper stories of each ran a balcony, or rather a terraced garden, supported by columns, filled with flowering plants, and tenanted by many kinds of tame birds.

From the square branched several streets, all broad and brilliantly lighted, and ascending up the eminence on either side. In my excursions in the town I was never allowed to go alone; Aph-Lin or his daughter was my habitual companion. In this community the adult Gy is seen walking with any young An as familiarly as if there were no difference of sex.

The retail shops are not very numerous; the persons who attend on a customer are all children of various ages, and exceedingly intelligent and courteous, but without the least touch of importunity or cringing. The shopkeeper himself might or might not be visible; when visible, he seemed rarely employed on any matter connected with his professional business; and yet he had taken to that business from special liking for it, and quite independently of his general sources of fortune.

The Ana of the community are, on the whole, an indolent set of beings after the active age of childhood. Whether by temperament or philosophy, they rank repose among the chief blessings of life. Indeed, when you take away from a human being the incentives to action which are found in cupidity or ambition, it seems to me no wonder that he rests quiet.

In their ordinary movements they prefer the use of their feet to that of their wings. But for their sports or (to indulge in a bold misuse of terms) their public 'promenades,' they employ the latter, also for the aerial dances I have described, as well as for visiting their country places, which are mostly placed on lofty heights; and, when still young, they prefer their wings for travel into the other regions of the Ana, to vehicular conveyances.

Those who accustom themselves to flight can fly, if less rapidly than some birds, yet from twenty-five to thirty miles an hour, and keep up that rate for five or six hours at a stretch. But the Ana generally, on reaching middle age, are not fond of rapid movements requiring violent exercise. Perhaps for this reason, as they hold a doctrine which our own physicians will doubtless approve—viz., that regular transpiration through the pores of the skin is essential to health, they habitually use the sweating-baths to which we give the name Turkish or Roman, succeeded by douches of perfumed waters. They have great faith in the salubrious virtue of certain perfumes.

It is their custom also, at stated but rare periods, perhaps four times a-year when in health, to use a bath charged with vril.*

* I once tried the effect of the vril bath. It was very similar in its invigorating powers to that of the baths at Gastein, the virtues of which are ascribed by many physicians to electricity; but though similar, the effect of the vril bath was more lasting.

They consider that this fluid, sparingly used, is a great sustainer of life; but used in excess, when in the normal state of health, rather tends to reaction and exhausted vitality. For nearly all their diseases, however, they resort to it as the chief assistant to nature in throwing off their complaint.

In their own way they are the most luxurious of people, but all their luxuries are innocent. They may be said to dwell in an atmosphere of music and fragrance. Every room has its mechanical contrivances for melodious sounds, usually tuned down to soft-murmured notes, which seem like sweet whispers from invisible spirits. They are too accustomed to these gentle sounds to find them a hindrance to conversation, nor, when alone, to reflection. But they have a notion that to breathe an air filled with continuous melody and perfume has necessarily an effect at once soothing and elevating upon the formation of character and the habits of thought. Though so temperate, and with total abstinence from other animal food than milk, and from all intoxicating drinks, they are delicate and dainty to an extreme in food and beverage; and in all their sports even the old exhibit a childlike gaiety. Happiness is the end at which they aim, not as the excitement of a moment, but as the prevailing condition of the entire existence; and regard for the happiness of each other is evinced by the exquisite amenity of their manners.

Their conformation of skull has marked differences from that of any known races in the upper world, though I cannot help thinking it a development, in the course of countless ages of the Brachycephalic type of the Age of Stone in Lyell's 'Elements of Geology,' C. X., p. 113, as compared with the Dolichocephalic type of the beginning of the Age of Iron, correspondent with that now so prevalent amongst us, and called the Celtic type. It has the same comparative massiveness of forehead, not receding like the Celtic—the same even roundness in the frontal organs; but it is far loftier in the apex, and far less pronounced in the hinder cranial hemisphere where phrenologists place the animal organs. To speak as a phrenologist, the cranium common to the Vril-ya has the organs of weight, number, tune, form, order, causality, very largely developed; that of construction much more pronounced than that of ideality. Those which are called the moral organs, such as conscientiousness and benevolence, are amazingly full; amativeness and combativeness are both small; adhesiveness large; the organ of destructiveness (i.e., of determined clearance of intervening obstacles) immense, but less than that of benevolence; and their philoprogenitiveness takes rather the character of compassion and tenderness to things that need aid or protection than of the animal love of offspring. I never met with one person deformed or misshapen. The beauty of their countenances is not only in symmetry of feature, but in a smoothness of surface, which continues without line or wrinkle to the extreme of old age, and a serene sweetness of expression, combined with that majesty which seems to come from consciousness of power and the freedom of all terror, physical or moral. It is that very sweetness, combined with that majesty, which inspired in a beholder like myself, accustomed to strive with the passions of mankind, a sentiment of humiliation, of awe, of dread. It is such an expression as a painter might give to a demi-god, a genius, an angel. The males of the Vril-ya are entirely beardless; the Gy-ei sometimes, in old age, develop a small moustache.

I was surprised to find that the colour of their skin was not uniformly that which I had remarked in those individuals whom I had first encountered,—some being much fairer, and even with blue eyes, and hair of a deep golden auburn, though still of complexions warmer or richer in tone than persons in the north of Europe.

I was told that this admixture of colouring arose from intermarriage with other and more distant tribes of the Vril-ya, who, whether by the accident of climate or early distinction of race, were of fairer hues than the tribes of which this community formed one. It was considered that the dark-red skin showed the most ancient family of Ana; but they attached no sentiment of pride to that antiquity, and, on the contrary, believed their present excellence of breed came from frequent crossing with other families differing, yet akin; and they encourage such intermarriages, always provided that it be with the Vril-ya nations. Nations which, not conforming their manners and institutions to those of the Vril-ya, nor indeed held capable of acquiring the powers over the vril agencies which it had taken them generations to attain and transmit, were regarded with more disdain than the citizens of New York regard the negroes.

I learned from Zee, who had more lore in all matters than any male with whom I was brought into familiar converse, that the superiority of the Vril-ya was supposed to have originated in the intensity of their earlier struggles against obstacles in nature amidst the localities in which they had first settled. "Wherever," said Zee, moralising, "wherever goes on that early process in the history of civilisation, by which life is made a struggle, in which the individual has to put forth all his powers to compete with his fellow, we invariably find this result—viz., since in the competition a vast number must perish, nature selects for preservation only the strongest specimens. With our race, therefore, even before the discovery of vril, only the highest organisations were preserved; and there is among our ancient books a legend, once popularly believed, that we were driven from a region that seems to denote the world you come from, in order to perfect our condition and attain to the purest elimination of our species by the severity of the struggles our forefathers underwent; and that, when our education shall become finally completed, we are destined to return to the upper world, and supplant all the inferior races now existing therein."

Aph-Lin and Zee often conversed with me in private upon the political and social conditions of that upper world, in which Zee so philosophically assumed that the inhabitants were to be exterminated one day or other by the advent of the Vril-ya. They found in my accounts,—in which I continued to do all I could (without launching into falsehoods so positive that they would have been easily detected by the shrewdness of my listeners) to present our powers and ourselves in the most flattering point of view,—perpetual subjects of comparison between our most civilised populations and the meaner subterranean races which they considered hopelessly plunged in barbarism, and doomed to gradual if certain extinction. But they both agreed in desiring to conceal from their community all premature opening into the regions lighted by the sun; both were humane, and shrunk from the thought of annihilating so many millions of creatures; and the pictures I drew of our life, highly coloured as they were, saddened them. In vain I boasted of our great men—poets, philosophers, orators, generals—and defied the Vril-ya to produce their equals. "Alas," said Zee, "this predominance of the few over the many is the surest and most fatal sign of a race incorrigibly savage. See you not that the primary condition of mortal happiness consists in the extinction of that strife and competition between individuals, which, no matter what forms of government they adopt, render the many subordinate to the few, destroy real liberty to the individual, whatever may be the nominal liberty of the state, and annul that calm of existence, without which, felicity, mental or bodily, cannot be attained? Our notion is, that the more we can assimilate life to the existence which our noblest ideas can conceive to be that of spirits on the other side of the grave, why, the more we approximate to a divine happiness here, and the more easily we glide into the conditions of being hereafter. For, surely, all we can imagine of the life of gods, or of blessed immortals, supposes the absence of self-made cares and contentious passions, such as avarice and ambition. It seems to us that it must be a life of serene tranquility, not indeed without active occupations to the intellectual or spiritual powers, but occupations, of whatsoever nature they be, congenial to the idiosyncrasies of each, not forced and repugnant—a life gladdened by the untrammelled interchange of gentle affections, in which the moral atmosphere utterly kills hate and vengeance, and strife and rivalry. Such is the political state to which all the tribes and families of the Vril-ya seek to attain, and towards that goal all our theories of government are shaped. You see how utterly opposed is such a progress to that of the uncivilised nations from which you come, and which aim at a systematic perpetuity of troubles, and cares, and warring passions aggravated more and more as their progress storms its way onward. The most powerful of all the races in our world, beyond the pale of the Vril-ya, esteems itself the best governed of all political societies, and to have reached in that respect the extreme end at which political wisdom can arrive, so that the other nations should tend more or less to copy it. It has established, on its broadest base, the Koom-Posh—viz., the government of the ignorant upon the principle of being the most numerous. It has placed the supreme bliss in the vying with each other in all things, so that the evil passions are never in repose—vying for power, for wealth, for eminence of some kind; and in this rivalry it is horrible to hear the vituperation, the slanders, and calumnies which even the best and mildest among them heap on each other without remorse or shame."

"Some years ago," said Aph-Lin, "I visited this people, and their misery and degradation were the more appalling because they were always boasting of their felicity and grandeur as compared with the rest of their species. And there is no hope that this people, which evidently resembles your own, can improve, because all their notions tend to further deterioration. They desire to enlarge their dominion more and more, in direct antagonism to the truth that, beyond a very limited range, it is impossible to secure to a community the happiness which belongs to a well-ordered family; and the more they mature a system by which a few individuals are heated and swollen to a size above the standard slenderness of the millions, the more they chuckle and exact, and cry out, 'See by what great exceptions to the common littleness of our race we prove the magnificent results of our system!'"

"In fact," resumed Zee, "if the wisdom of human life be to approximate to the serene equality of immortals, there can be no more direct flying off into the opposite direction than a system which aims at carrying to the utmost the inequalities and turbulences of mortals. Nor do I see how, by any forms of religious belief, mortals, so acting, could fit themselves even to appreciate the joys of immortals to which they still expect to be transferred by the mere act of dying. On the contrary, minds accustomed to place happiness in things so much the reverse of godlike, would find the happiness of gods exceedingly dull, and would long to get back to a world in which they could quarrel with each other."

Chapter XVI.

I have spoken so much of the Vril Staff that my reader may expect me to describe it. This I cannot do accurately, for I was never allowed to handle it for fear of some terrible accident occasioned by my ignorance of its use; and I have no doubt that it requires much skill and practice in the exercise of its various powers. It is hollow, and has in the handle several stops, keys, or springs by which its force can be altered, modified, or directed—so that by one process it destroys, by another it heals—by one it can rend the rock, by another disperse the vapour—by one it affects bodies, by another it can exercise a certain influence over minds. It is usually carried in the convenient size of a walking-staff, but it has slides by which it can be lengthened or shortened at will. When used for special purposes, the upper part rests in the hollow of the palm with the fore and middle fingers protruded. I was assured, however, that its power was not equal in all, but proportioned to the amount of certain vril properties in the wearer in affinity, or 'rapport' with the purposes to be effected. Some were more potent to destroy, others to heal, &c.; much also depended on the calm and steadiness of volition in the manipulator. They assert that the full exercise of vril power can only be acquired by the constitutional temperament—i.e., by hereditarily transmitted organisation—and that a female infant of four years old belonging to the Vril-ya races can accomplish feats which a life spent in its practice would not enable the strongest and most skilled mechanician, born out of the pale of the Vril-ya to achieve. All these wands are not equally complicated; those intrusted to children are much simpler than those borne by sages of either sex, and constructed with a view to the special object on which the children are employed; which as I have before said, is among the youngest children the most destructive. In the wands of wives and mothers the correlative destroying force is usually abstracted, the healing power fully charged. I wish I could say more in detail of this singular conductor of the vril fluid, but its machinery is as exquisite as its effects are marvellous.

I should say, however, that this people have invented certain tubes by which the vril fluid can be conducted towards the object it is meant to destroy, throughout a distance almost indefinite; at least I put it modestly when I say from 500 to 1000 miles. And their mathematical science as applied to such purpose is so nicely accurate, that on the report of some observer in an air-boat, any member of the vril department can estimate unerringly the nature of intervening obstacles, the height to which the projectile instrument should be raised, and the extent to which it should be charged, so as to reduce to ashes within a space of time too short for me to venture to specify it, a capital twice as vast as London.

Certainly these Ana are wonderful mathematicians—wonderful for the adaptation of the inventive faculty to practical uses.

I went with my host and his daughter Zee over the great public museum, which occupies a wing in the College of Sages, and in which are hoarded, as curious specimens of the ignorant and blundering experiments of ancient times, many contrivances on which we pride ourselves as recent achievements. In one department, carelessly thrown aside as obsolete lumber, are tubes for destroying life by metallic balls and an inflammable powder, on the principle of our cannons and catapults, and even still more murderous than our latest improvements.

My host spoke of these with a smile of contempt, such as an artillery officer might bestow on the bows and arrows of the Chinese. In another department there were models of vehicles and vessels worked by steam, and of an air-balloon which might have been constructed by Montgolfier. "Such," said Zee, with an air of meditative wisdom—"such were the feeble triflings with nature of our savage forefathers, ere they had even a glimmering perception of the properties of vril!"

This young Gy was a magnificent specimen of the muscular force to which the females of her country attain. Her features were beautiful, like those of all her race: never in the upper world have I seen a face so grand and so faultless, but her devotion to the severer studies had given to her countenance an expression of abstract thought which rendered it somewhat stern when in repose; and such a sternness became formidable when observed in connection with her ample shoulders and lofty stature. She was tall even for a Gy, and I saw her lift up a cannon as easily as I could lift a pocket-pistol. Zee inspired me with a profound terror—a terror which increased when we came into a department of the museum appropriated to models of contrivances worked by the agency of vril; for here, merely by a certain play of her vril staff, she herself standing at a distance, she put into movement large and weighty substances. She seemed to endow them with intelligence, and to make them comprehend and obey her command. She set complicated pieces of machinery into movement, arrested the movement or continued it, until, within an incredibly short time, various kinds of raw material were reproduced as symmetrical works of art, complete and perfect. Whatever effect mesmerism or electro-biology produces over the nerves and muscles of animated objects, this young Gy produced by the motions of her slender rod over the springs and wheels of lifeless mechanism.

When I mentioned to my companions my astonishment at this influence over inanimate matter—while owning that, in our world, I had witnessed phenomena which showed that over certain living organisations certain other living organisations could establish an influence genuine in itself, but often exaggerated by credulity or craft—Zee, who was more interested in such subjects than her father, bade me stretch forth my hand, and then, placing it beside her own, she called my attention to certain distinctions of type and character. In the first place, the thumb of the Gy (and, as I afterwards noticed, of all that race, male or female) was much larger, at once longer and more massive, than is found with our species above ground. There is almost, in this, as great a difference as there is between the thumb of a man and that of a gorilla. Secondly, the palm is proportionally thicker than ours—the texture of the skin infinitely finer and softer— its average warmth is greater. More remarkable than all this, is a visible nerve, perceptible under the skin, which starts from the wrist skirting the ball of the thumb, and branching, fork-like, at the roots of the fore and middle fingers. "With your slight formation of thumb," said the philosophical young Gy, "and with the absence of the nerve which you find more or less developed in the hands of our race, you can never achieve other than imperfect and feeble power over the agency of vril; but so far as the nerve is concerned, that is not found in the hands of our earliest progenitors, nor in those of the ruder tribes without the pale of the Vril-ya. It has been slowly developed in the course of generations, commencing in the early achievements, and increasing with the continuous exercise, of the vril power; therefore, in the course of one or two thousand years, such a nerve may possibly be engendered in those higher beings of your race, who devote themselves to that paramount science through which is attained command over all the subtler forces of nature permeated by vril. But when you talk of matter as something in itself inert and motionless, your parents or tutors surely cannot have left you so ignorant as not to know that no form of matter is motionless and inert: every particle is constantly in motion and constantly acted upon by agencies, of which heat is the most apparent and rapid, but vril the most subtle, and, when skilfully wielded, the most powerful. So that, in fact, the current launched by my hand and guided by my will does but render quicker and more potent the action which is eternally at work upon every particle of matter, however inert and stubborn it may seem. If a heap of metal be not capable of originating a thought of its own, yet, through its internal susceptibility to movement, it obtains the power to receive the thought of the intellectual agent at work on it; by which, when conveyed with a sufficient force of the vril power, it is as much compelled to obey as if it were displaced by a visible bodily force. It is animated for the time being by the soul thus infused into it, so that one may almost say that it lives and reasons. Without this we could not make our automata supply the place of servants."

I was too much in awe of the thews and the learning of the young Gy to hazard the risk of arguing with her. I had read somewhere in my schoolboy days that a wise man, disputing with a Roman Emperor, suddenly drew in his horns; and when the emperor asked him whether he had nothing further to say on his side of the question, replied, "Nay, Caesar, there is no arguing against a reasoner who commands ten legions."

Though I had a secret persuasion that, whatever the real effects of vril upon matter, Mr. Faraday could have proved her a very shallow philosopher as to its extent or its causes, I had no doubt that Zee could have brained all the Fellows of the Royal Society, one after the other, with a blow of her fist. Every sensible man knows that it is useless to argue with any ordinary female upon matters he comprehends; but to argue with a Gy seven feet high upon the mysteries of vril,—as well argue in a desert, and with a simoon!

Amid the various departments to which the vast building of the College of Sages was appropriated, that which interested me most was devoted to the archaeology of the Vril-ya, and comprised a very ancient collection of portraits. In these the pigments and groundwork employed were of so durable a nature that even pictures said to be executed at dates as remote as those in the earliest annals of the Chinese, retained much freshness of colour. In examining this collection, two things especially struck me:—first, that the pictures said to be between 6000 and 7000 years old were of a much higher degree of art than any produced within the last 3000 or 4000 years; and, second, that the portraits within the former period much more resembled our own upper world and European types of countenance. Some of them, indeed reminded me of the Italian heads which look out from the canvases of Titian—speaking of ambition or craft, of care or of grief, with furrows in which the passions have passed with iron ploughshare. These were the countenances of men who had lived in struggle and conflict before the discovery of the latent forces of vril had changed the character of society—men who had fought with each other for power or fame as we in the upper world fight.

The type of face began to evince a marked change about a thousand years after the vril revolution, becoming then, with each generation, more serene, and in that serenity more terribly distinct from the faces of labouring and sinful men; while in proportion as the beauty and the grandeur of the countenance itself became more fully developed, the art of the painter became more tame and monotonous.

But the greatest curiosity in the collection was that of three portraits belonging to the pre-historical age, and, according to mythical tradition, taken by the orders of a philosopher, whose origin and attributes were as much mixed up with symbolical fable as those of an Indian Budh or a Greek Prometheus.

From this mysterious personage, at once a sage and a hero, all the principal sections of the Vril-ya race pretend to trace a common origin.

The portraits are of the philosopher himself, of his grandfather, and great-grandfather. They are all at full length. The philosopher is attired in a long tunic which seems to form a loose suit of scaly armour, borrowed, perhaps, from some fish or reptile, but the feet and hands are exposed: the digits in both are wonderfully long, and webbed. He has little or no perceptible throat, and a low receding forehead, not at all the ideal of a sage's. He has bright brown prominent eyes, a very wide mouth and high cheekbones, and a muddy complexion. According to tradition, this philosopher had lived to a patriarchal age, extending over many centuries, and he remembered distinctly in middle life his grandfather as surviving, and in childhood his great-grandfather; the portrait of the first he had taken, or caused to be taken, while yet alive—that of the latter was taken from his effigies in mummy. The portrait of his grandfather had the features and aspect of the philosopher, only much more exaggerated: he was not dressed, and the colour of his body was singular; the breast and stomach yellow, the shoulders and legs of a dull bronze hue: the great-grandfather was a magnificent specimen of the Batrachian genus, a Giant Frog, 'pur et simple.'

Among the pithy sayings which, according to tradition, the philosopher bequeathed to posterity in rhythmical form and sententious brevity, this is notably recorded: "Humble yourselves, my descendants; the father of your race was a 'twat' (tadpole): exalt yourselves, my descendants, for it was the same Divine Thought which created your father that develops itself in exalting you."

Aph-Lin told me this fable while I gazed on the three Batrachian portraits. I said in reply: "You make a jest of my supposed ignorance and credulity as an uneducated Tish, but though these horrible daubs may be of great antiquity, and were intended, perhaps, for some rude caracature, I presume that none of your race even in the less enlightened ages, ever believed that the great-grandson of a Frog became a sententious philosopher; or that any section, I will not say of the lofty Vril-ya, but of the meanest varieties of the human race, had its origin in a Tadpole."

"Pardon me," answered Aph-Lin: "in what we call the Wrangling or Philosophical Period of History, which was at its height about seven thousand years ago, there was a very distinguished naturalist, who proved to the satisfaction of numerous disciples such analogical and anatomical agreements in structure between an An and a Frog, as to show that out of the one must have developed the other. They had some diseases in common; they were both subject to the same parasitical worms in the intestines; and, strange to say, the An has, in his structure, a swimming-bladder, no longer of any use to him, but which is a rudiment that clearly proves his descent from a Frog. Nor is there any argument against this theory to be found in the relative difference of size, for there are still existent in our world Frogs of a size and stature not inferior to our own, and many thousand years ago they appear to have been still larger."

"I understand that," said I, "because Frogs this enormous are, according to our eminent geologists, who perhaps saw them in dreams, said to have been distinguished inhabitants of the upper world before the Deluge; and such Frogs are exactly the creatures likely to have flourished in the lakes and morasses of your subterranean regions. But pray, proceed."

"In the Wrangling Period of History, whatever one sage asserted another sage was sure to contradict. In fact, it was a maxim in that age, that the human reason could only be sustained aloft by being tossed to and fro in the perpetual motion of contradiction; and therefore another sect of philosophers maintained the doctrine that the An was not the descendant of the Frog, but that the Frog was clearly the improved development of the An. The shape of the Frog, taken generally, was much more symmetrical than that of the An; beside the beautiful conformation of its lower limbs, its flanks and shoulders the majority of the Ana in that day were almost deformed, and certainly ill-shaped. Again, the Frog had the power to live alike on land and in water—a mighty privilege, partaking of a spiritual essence denied to the An, since the disuse of his swimming-bladder clearly proves his degeneration from a higher development of species. Again, the earlier races of the Ana seem to have been covered with hair, and, even to a comparatively recent date, hirsute bushes deformed the very faces of our ancestors, spreading wild over their cheeks and chins, as similar bushes, my poor Tish, spread wild over yours. But the object of the higher races of the Ana through countless generations has been to erase all vestige of connection with hairy vertebrata, and they have gradually eliminated that debasing capillary excrement by the law of sexual selection; the Gy-ei naturally preferring youth or the beauty of smooth faces. But the degree of the Frog in the scale of the vertebrata is shown in this, that he has no hair at all, not even on his head. He was born to that hairless perfection which the most beautiful of the Ana, despite the culture of incalculable ages, have not yet attained. The wonderful complication and delicacy of a Frog's nervous system and arterial circulation were shown by this school to be more susceptible of enjoyment than our inferior, or at least simpler, physical frame allows us to be. The examination of a Frog's hand, if I may use that expression, accounted for its keener susceptibility to love, and to social life in general. In fact, gregarious and amatory as are the Ana, Frogs are still more so. In short, these two schools raged against each other; one asserting the An to be the perfected type of the Frog; the other that the Frog was the highest development of the An. The moralists were divided in opinion with the naturalists, but the bulk of them sided with the Frog-preference school. They said, with much plausibility, that in moral conduct (viz., in the adherence to rules best adapted to the health and welfare of the individual and the community) there could be no doubt of the vast superiority of the Frog. All history showed the wholesale immorality of the human race, the complete disregard, even by the most renowned amongst them, of the laws which they acknowledged to be essential to their own and the general happiness and wellbeing. But the severest critic of the Frog race could not detect in their manners a single aberration from the moral law tacitly recognised by themselves. And what, after all, can be the profit of civilisation if superiority in moral conduct be not the aim for which it strives, and the test by which its progress should be judged?

"In fine, the adherents of this theory presumed that in some remote period the Frog race had been the improved development of the Human; but that, from some causes which defied rational conjecture, they had not maintained their original position in the scale of nature; while the Ana, though of inferior organisation, had, by dint less of their virtues than their vices, such as ferocity and cunning, gradually acquired ascendancy, much as among the human race itself tribes utterly barbarous have, by superiority in similar vices, utterly destroyed or reduced into insignificance tribes originally excelling them in mental gifts and culture. Unhappily these disputes became involved with the religious notions of that age; and as society was then administered under the government of the Koom-Posh, who, being the most ignorant, were of course the most inflammable class—the multitude took the whole question out of the hands of the philosophers; political chiefs saw that the Frog dispute, so taken up by the populace, could become a most valuable instrument of their ambition; and for not less than one thousand years war and massacre prevailed, during which period the philosophers on both sides were butchered, and the government of Koom-Posh itself was happily brought to an end by the ascendancy of a family that clearly established its descent from the aboriginal tadpole, and furnished despotic rulers to the various nations of the Ana. These despots finally disappeared, at least from our communities, as the discovery of vril led to the tranquil institutions under which flourish all the races of the Vril-ya."

"And do no wranglers or philosophers now exist to revive the dispute; or do they all recognise the origin of your race in the tadpole?"

"Nay, such disputes," said Zee, with a lofty smile, "belong to the Pah-bodh of the dark ages, and now only serve for the amusement of infants. When we know the elements out of which our bodies are composed, elements in common to the humblest vegetable plants, can it signify whether the All-Wise combined those elements out of one form more than another, in order to create that in which He has placed the capacity to receive the idea of Himself, and all the varied grandeurs of intellect to which that idea gives birth? The An in reality commenced to exist as An with the donation of that capacity, and, with that capacity, the sense to acknowledge that, however through the countless ages his race may improve in wisdom, it can never combine the elements at its command into the form of a tadpole."

"You speak well, Zee," said Aph-Lin; "and it is enough for us shortlived mortals to feel a reasonable assurance that whether the origin of the An was a tadpole or not, he is no more likely to become a tadpole again than the institutions of the Vril-ya are likely to relapse into the heaving quagmire and certain strife-rot of a Koom-Posh."

Chapter XVII.

The Vril-ya, being excluded from all sight of the heavenly bodies, and having no other difference between night and day than that which they deem it convenient to make for themselves,—do not, of course, arrive at their divisions of time by the same process that we do; but I found it easy by the aid of my watch, which I luckily had about me, to compute their time with great nicety. I reserve for a future work on the science and literature of the Vril-ya, should I live to complete it, all details as to the manner in which they arrive at their rotation of time; and content myself here with saying, that in point of duration, their year differs very slightly from ours, but that the divisions of their year are by no means the same. Their day, (including what we call night) consists of twenty hours of our time, instead of twenty-four, and of course their year comprises the correspondent increase in the number of days by which it is summed up. They subdivide the twenty hours of their day thus—eight hours,* called the "Silent Hours," for repose; eight hours, called the "Earnest Time," for the pursuits and occupations of life; and four hours called the "Easy Time" (with which what I may term their day closes), allotted to festivities, sport, recreation, or family converse, according to their several tastes and inclinations.

* For the sake of convenience, I adopt the word hours, days, years, &c., in any general reference to subdivisions of time among the Vril-ya; those terms but loosely corresponding, however, with such subdivisions.

But, in truth, out of doors there is no night. They maintain, both in the streets and in the surrounding country, to the limits of their territory, the same degree of light at all hours. Only, within doors, they lower it to a soft twilight during the Silent Hours. They have a great horror of perfect darkness, and their lights are never wholly extinguished. On occasions of festivity they continue the duration of full light, but equally keep note of the distinction between night and day, by mechanical contrivances which answer the purpose of our clocks and watches. They are very fond of music; and it is by music that these chronometers strike the principal division of time. At every one of their hours, during their day, the sounds coming from all the time-pieces in their public buildings, and caught up, as it were, by those of houses or hamlets scattered amidst the landscapes without the city, have an effect singularly sweet, and yet singularly solemn. But during the Silent Hours these sounds are so subdued as to be only faintly heard by a waking ear. They have no change of seasons, and, at least on the territory of this tribe, the atmosphere seemed to me very equable, warm as that of an Italian summer, and humid rather than dry; in the forenoon usually very still, but at times invaded by strong blasts from the rocks that made the borders of their domain. But time is the same to them for sowing or reaping as in the Golden Isles of the ancient poets. At the same moment you see the younger plants in blade or bud, the older in ear or fruit. All fruit-bearing plants, however, after fruitage, either shed or change the colour of their leaves. But that which interested me most in reckoning up their divisions of time was the ascertainment of the average duration of life amongst them. I found on minute inquiry that this very considerably exceeded the term allotted to us on the upper earth. What seventy years are to us, one hundred years are to them. Nor is this the only advantage they have over us in longevity, for as few among us attain to the age of seventy, so, on the contrary, few among them die before the age of one hundred; and they enjoy a general degree of health and vigour which makes life itself a blessing even to the last. Various causes contribute to this result: the absence of all alcoholic stimulants; temperance in food; more especially, perhaps, a serenity of mind undisturbed by anxious occupations and eager passions. They are not tormented by our avarice or our ambition; they appear perfectly indifferent even to the desire of fame; they are capable of great affection, but their love shows itself in a tender and cheerful complaisance, and, while forming their happiness, seems rarely, if ever, to constitute their woe. As the Gy is sure only to marry where she herself fixes her choice, and as here, not less than above ground, it is the female on whom the happiness of home depends; so the Gy, having chosen the mate she prefers to all others, is lenient to his faults, consults his humours, and does her best to secure his attachment. The death of a beloved one is of course with them, as with us, a cause for sorrow; but not only is death with them so much more rare before that age in which it becomes a release, but when it does occur the survivor takes much more consolation than, I am afraid, the generality of us do, in the certainty of reunion in another and yet happier life.

All these causes, then, concur to their healthful and enjoyable longevity, though, no doubt, much also must be owing to hereditary organisation. According to their records, however, in those earlier stages of their society when they lived in communities resembling ours, agitated by fierce competition, their lives were considerably shorter, and their maladies more numerous and grave. They themselves say that the duration of life, too, has increased, and is still on the increase, since their discovery of the invigorating and medicinal properties of vril, applied for remedial purposes. They have few professional and regular practitioners of medicine, and these are chiefly Gy-ei, who, especially if widowed and childless, find great delight in the healing art, and even undertake surgical operations in those cases required by accident, or, more rarely, by disease.

They have their diversions and entertainments, and, during the Easy Time of their day, they are wont to assemble in great numbers for those winged sports in the air which I have already described. They have also public halls for music, and even theatres, at which are performed pieces that appeared to me somewhat to resemble the plays of the Chinese—dramas that are thrown back into distant times for their events and personages, in which all classic unities are outrageously violated, and the hero, in once scene a child, in the next is an old man, and so forth. These plays are of very ancient composition, and their stories cast in remote times. They appeared to me very dull, on the whole, but were relieved by startling mechanical contrivances, and a kind of farcical broad humour, and detached passages of great vigour and power expressed in language highly poetical, but somewhat overcharged with metaphor and trope. In fine, they seemed to me very much what the plays of Shakespeare seemed to a Parisian in the time of Louis XV., or perhaps to an Englishman in the reign of Charles II.

The audience, of which the Gy-ei constituted the chief portion, appeared to enjoy greatly the representation of these dramas, which, for so sedate and majestic a race of females, surprised me, till I observed that all the performers were under the age of adolescence, and conjectured truly that the mothers and sisters came to please their children and brothers.

I have said that these dramas are of great antiquity. No new plays, indeed no imaginative works sufficiently important to survive their immediate day, appear to have been composed for several generations. In fact, though there is no lack of new publications, and they have even what may be called newspapers, these are chiefly devoted to mechanical science, reports of new inventions, announcements respecting various details of business—in short, to practical matters. Sometimes a child writes a little tale of adventure, or a young Gy vents her amorous hopes or fears in a poem; but these effusions are of very little merit, and are seldom read except by children and maiden Gy-ei. The most interesting works of a purely literary character are those of explorations and travels into other regions of this nether world, which are generally written by young emigrants, and are read with great avidity by the relations and friends they have left behind.

I could not help expressing to Aph-Lin my surprise that a community in which mechanical science had made so marvellous a progress, and in which intellectual civilisation had exhibited itself in realising those objects for the happiness of the people, which the political philosophers above ground had, after ages of struggle, pretty generally agreed to consider unattainable visions, should, nevertheless, be so wholly without a contemporaneous literature, despite the excellence to which culture had brought a language at once so rich and simple, vigourous and musical.

My host replied—"Do you not perceive that a literature such as you mean would be wholly incompatible with that perfection of social or political felicity at which you do us the honour to think we have arrived? We have at last, after centuries of struggle, settled into a form of government with which we are content, and in which, as we allow no differences of rank, and no honours are paid to administrators distinguishing them from others, there is no stimulus given to individual ambition. No one would read works advocating theories that involved any political or social change, and therefore no one writes them. If now and then an An feels himself dissatisfied with our tranquil mode of life, he does not attack it; he goes away. Thus all that part of literature (and to judge by the ancient books in our public libraries, it was once a very large part), which relates to speculative theories on society is become utterly extinct. Again, formerly there was a vast deal written respecting the attributes and essence of the All-Good, and the arguments for and against a future state; but now we all recognise two facts, that there IS a Divine Being, and there IS a future state, and we all equally agree that if we wrote our fingers to the bone, we could not throw any light upon the nature and conditions of that future state, or quicken our apprehensions of the attributes and essence of that Divine Being. Thus another part of literature has become also extinct, happily for our race; for in the time when so much was written on subjects which no one could determine, people seemed to live in a perpetual state of quarrel and contention. So, too, a vast part of our ancient literature consists of historical records of wars an revolutions during the times when the Ana lived in large and turbulent societies, each seeking aggrandisement at the expense of the other. You see our serene mode of life now; such it has been for ages. We have no events to chronicle. What more of us can be said than that, 'they were born, they were happy, they died?' Coming next to that part of literature which is more under the control of the imagination, such as what we call Glaubsila, or colloquially 'Glaubs,' and you call poetry, the reasons for its decline amongst us are abundantly obvious.

"We find, by referring to the great masterpieces in that department of literature which we all still read with pleasure, but of which none would tolerate imitations, that they consist in the portraiture of passions which we no longer experience—ambition, vengeance, unhallowed love, the thirst for warlike renown, and suchlike. The old poets lived in an atmosphere impregnated with these passions, and felt vividly what they expressed glowingly. No one can express such passions now, for no one can feel them, or meet with any sympathy in his readers if he did. Again, the old poetry has a main element in its dissection of those complex mysteries of human character which conduce to abnormal vices and crimes, or lead to signal and extraordinary virtues. But our society, having got rid of temptations to any prominent vices and crimes, has necessarily rendered the moral average so equal, that there are no very salient virtues. Without its ancient food of strong passions, vast crimes, heroic excellences, poetry therefore is, if not actually starved to death, reduced to a very meagre diet. There is still the poetry of description—description of rocks, and trees, and waters, and common household life; and our young Gy-ei weave much of this insipid kind of composition into their love verses."

"Such poetry," said I, "might surely be made very charming; and we have critics amongst us who consider it a higher kind than that which depicts the crimes, or analyses the passions, of man. At all events, poetry of the inspired kind you mention is a poetry that nowadays commands more readers than any other among the people I have left above ground."

"Possibly; but then I suppose the writers take great pains with the language they employ, and devote themselves to the culture and polish of words and rhythms of an art?"

"Certainly they do: all great poets do that. Though the gift of poetry may be inborn, the gift requires as much care to make it available as a block of metal does to be made into one of your engines."

"And doubtless your poets have some incentive to bestow all those pains upon such verbal prettinesses?"

"Well, I presume their instinct of song would make them sing as the bird does; but to cultivate the song into verbal or artificial prettiness, probably does need an inducement from without, and our poets find it in the love of fame—perhaps, now and then, in the want of money."

"Precisely so. But in our society we attach fame to nothing which man, in that moment of his duration which is called 'life,' can perform. We should soon lose that equality which constitutes the felicitous essence of our commonwealth if we selected any individual for pre-eminent praise: pre-eminent praise would confer pre-eminent power, and the moment it were given, evil passions, now dormant, would awake: other men would immediately covet praise, then would arise envy, and with envy hate, and with hate calumny and persecution. Our history tells us that most of the poets and most of the writers who, in the old time, were favoured with the greatest praise, were also assailed by the greatest vituperation, and even, on the whole, rendered very unhappy, partly by the attacks of jealous rivals, partly by the diseased mental constitution which an acquired sensitiveness to praise and to blame tends to engender. As for the stimulus of want; in the first place, no man in our community knows the goad of poverty; and, secondly, if he did, almost every occupation would be more lucrative than writing.

"Our public libraries contain all the books of the past which time has preserved; those books, for the reasons above stated, are infinitely better than any can write nowadays, and they are open to all to read without cost. We are not such fools as to pay for reading inferior books, when we can read superior books for nothing."

"With us, novelty has an attraction; and a new book, if bad, is read when an old book, though good, is neglected."

"Novelty, to barbarous states of society struggling in despair for something better, has no doubt an attraction, denied to us, who see nothing to gain in novelties; but after all, it is observed by one of our great authors four thousand years ago, that 'he who studies old books will always find in them something new, and he who reads new books will always find in them something old.' But to return to the question you have raised, there being then amongst us no stimulus to painstaking labour, whether in desire of fame or in pressure of want, such as have the poetic temperament, no doubt vent it in song, as you say the bird sings; but for lack of elaborate culture it fails of an audience, and, failing of an audience, dies out, of itself, amidst the ordinary avocations of life."

"But how is it that these discouragements to the cultivation of literature do not operate against that of science?"

"Your question amazes me. The motive to science is the love of truth apart from all consideration of fame, and science with us too is devoted almost solely to practical uses, essential to our social conversation and the comforts of our daily life. No fame is asked by the inventor, and none is given to him; he enjoys an occupation congenial to his tastes, and needing no wear and tear of the passions. Man must have exercise for his mind as well as body; and continuous exercise, rather than violent, is best for both. Our most ingenious cultivators of science are, as a general rule, the longest lived and the most free from disease. Painting is an amusement to many, but the art is not what it was in former times, when the great painters in our various communities vied with each other for the prize of a golden crown, which gave them a social rank equal to that of the kings under whom they lived. You will thus doubtless have observed in our archaeological department how superior in point of art the pictures were several thousand years ago. Perhaps it is because music is, in reality, more allied to science than it is to poetry, that, of all the pleasurable arts, music is that which flourishes the most amongst us. Still, even in music the absence of stimulus in praise or fame has served to prevent any great superiority of one individual over another; and we rather excel in choral music, with the aid of our vast mechanical instruments, in which we make great use of the agency of water,* than in single performers."

* This may remind the student of Nero's invention of a musical machine, by which water was made to perform the part of an orchestra, and on which he was employed when the conspiracy against him broke out.

"We have had scarcely any original composer for some ages. Our favorite airs are very ancient in substance, but have admitted many complicated variations by inferior, though ingenious, musicians."

"Are there no political societies among the Ana which are animated by those passions, subjected to those crimes, and admitting those disparities in condition, in intellect, and in morality, which the state of your tribe, or indeed of the Vril-ya generally, has left behind in its progress to perfection? If so, among such societies perhaps Poetry and her sister arts still continue to be honoured and to improve?"

"There are such societies in remote regions, but we do not admit them within the pale of civilised communities; we scarcely even give them the name of Ana, and certainly not that of Vril-ya. They are savages, living chiefly in that low stage of being, Koom-Posh, tending necessarily to its own hideous dissolution in Glek-Nas. Their wretched existence is passed in perpetual contest and perpetual change. When they do not fight with their neighbours, they fight among themselves. They are divided into sections, which abuse, plunder, and sometimes murder each other, and on the most frivolous points of difference that would be unintelligible to us if we had not read history, and seen that we too have passed through the same early state of ignorance and barbarism. Any trifle is sufficient to set them together by the ears. They pretend to be all equals, and the more they have struggled to be so, by removing old distinctions, and starting afresh, the more glaring and intolerable the disparity becomes, because nothing in hereditary affections and associations is left to soften the one naked distinction between the many who have nothing and the few who have much. Of course the many hate the few, but without the few they could not live. The many are always assailing the few; sometimes they exterminate the few; but as soon as they have done so, a new few starts out of the many, and is harder to deal with than the old few. For where societies are large, and competition to have something is the predominant fever, there must be always many losers and few gainers. In short, they are savages groping their way in the dark towards some gleam of light, and would demand our commiseration for their infirmities, if, like all savages, they did not provoke their own destruction by their arrogance and cruelty. Can you imagine that creatures of this kind, armed only with such miserable weapons as you may see in our museum of antiquities, clumsy iron tubes charged with saltpetre, have more than once threatened with destruction a tribe of the Vril-ya, which dwells nearest to them, because they say they have thirty millions of population—and that tribe may have fifty thousand—if the latter do not accept their notions of Soc-Sec (money getting) on some trading principles which they have the impudence to call 'a law of civilisation'?"

"But thirty millions of population are formidable odds against fifty thousand!"

My host stared at me astonished. "Stranger," said he, "you could not have heard me say that this threatened tribe belongs to the Vril-ya; and it only waits for these savages to declare war, in order to commission some half-a-dozen small children to sweep away their whole population."

At these words I felt a thrill of horror, recognising much more affinity with "the savages" than I did with the Vril-ya, and remembering all I had said in praise of the glorious American institutions, which Aph-Lin stigmatised as Koom-Posh. Recovering my self-possession, I asked if there were modes of transit by which I could safely visit this temerarious and remote people.

"You can travel with safety, by vril agency, either along the ground or amid the air, throughout all the range of the communities with which we are allied and akin; but I cannot vouch for your safety in barbarous nations governed by different laws from ours; nations, indeed, so benighted, that there are among them large numbers who actually live by stealing from each other, and one could not with safety in the Silent Hours even leave the doors of one's own house open."

Here our conversation was interrupted by the entrance of Taee, who came to inform us that he, having been deputed to discover and destroy the enormous reptile which I had seen on my first arrival, had been on the watch for it ever since his visit to me, and had began to suspect that my eyes had deceived me, or that the creature had made its way through the cavities within the rocks to the wild regions in which dwelt its kindred race,—when it gave evidences of its whereabouts by a great devastation of the herbage bordering one of the lakes. "And," said Taee, "I feel sure that within that lake it is now hiding. So," (turning to me) "I thought it might amuse you to accompany me to see the way we destroy such unpleasant visitors." As I looked at the face of the young child, and called to mind the enormous size of the creature he proposed to exterminate, I felt myself shudder with fear for him, and perhaps fear for myself, if I accompanied him in such a chase. But my curiosity to witness the destructive effects of the boasted vril, and my unwillingness to lower myself in the eyes of an infant by betraying apprehensions of personal safety, prevailed over my first impulse. Accordingly, I thanked Taee for his courteous consideration for my amusement, and professed my willingness to set out with him on so diverting an enterprise.

Chapter XVIII.

As Taee and myself, on quitting the town, and leaving to the left the main road which led to it, struck into the fields, the strange and solemn beauty of the landscape, lighted up, by numberless lamps, to the verge of the horizon, fascinated my eyes, and rendered me for some time an inattentive listener to the talk of my companion.

Along our way various operations of agriculture were being carried on by machinery, the forms of which were new to me, and for the most part very graceful; for among these people art being so cultivated for the sake of mere utility, exhibits itself in adorning or refining the shapes of useful objects. Precious metals and gems are so profuse among them, that they are lavished on things devoted to purposes the most commonplace; and their love of utility leads them to beautify its tools, and quickens their imagination in a way unknown to themselves.

In all service, whether in or out of doors, they make great use of automaton figures, which are so ingenious, and so pliant to the operations of vril, that they actually seem gifted with reason. It was scarcely possible to distinguish the figures I beheld, apparently guiding or superintending the rapid movements of vast engines, from human forms endowed with thought.

By degrees, as we continued to walk on, my attention became roused by the lively and acute remarks of my companion. The intelligence of the children among this race is marvellously precocious, perhaps from the habit of having intrusted to them, at so early an age, the toils and responsibilities of middle age. Indeed, in conversing with Taee, I felt as if talking with some superior and observant man of my own years. I asked him if he could form any estimate of the number of communities into which the race of the Vril-ya is subdivided.

"Not exactly," he said, "because they multiply, of course, every year as the surplus of each community is drafted off. But I heard my father say that, according to the last report, there were a million and a half of communities speaking our language, and adopting our institutions and forms of life and government; but, I believe, with some differences, about which you had better ask Zee. She knows more than most of the Ana do. An An cares less for things that do not concern him than a Gy does; the Gy-ei are inquisitive creatures."

"Does each community restrict itself to the same number of families or amount of population that you do?"

"No; some have much smaller populations, some have larger—varying according to the extent of the country they appropriate, or to the degree of excellence to which they have brought their machinery. Each community sets its own limit according to circumstances, taking care always that there shall never arise any class of poor by the pressure of population upon the productive powers of the domain; and that no state shall be too large for a government resembling that of a single well-ordered family. I imagine that no vril community exceeds thirty-thousand households. But, as a general rule, the smaller the community, provided there be hands enough to do justice to the capacities of the territory it occupies, the richer each individual is, and the larger the sum contributed to the general treasury,—above all, the happier and the more tranquil is the whole political body, and the more perfect the products of its industry. The state which all tribes of the Vril-ya acknowledge to be the highest in civilisation, and which has brought the vril force to its fullest development, is perhaps the smallest. It limits itself to four thousand families; but every inch of its territory is cultivated to the utmost perfection of garden ground; its machinery excels that of every other tribe, and there is no product of its industry in any department which is not sought for, at extraordinary prices, by each community of our race. All our tribes make this state their model, considering that we should reach the highest state of civilisation allowed to mortals if we could unite the greatest degree of happiness with the highest degree of intellectual achievement; and it is clear that the smaller the society the less difficult that will be. Ours is too large for it."

This reply set me thinking. I reminded myself of that little state of Athens, with only twenty thousand free citizens, and which to this day our mightiest nations regard as the supreme guide and model in all departments of intellect. But then Athens permitted fierce rivalry and perpetual change, and was certainly not happy. Rousing myself from the reverie into which these reflections had plunged me, I brought back our talk to the subjects connected with emigration.

"But," said I, "when, I suppose yearly, a certain number among you agree to quit home and found a new community elsewhere, they must necessarily be very few, and scarcely sufficient, even with the help of the machines they take with them, to clear the ground, and build towns, and form a civilised state with the comforts and luxuries in which they had been reared."

"You mistake. All the tribes of the Vril-ya are in constant communication with each other, and settle amongst themselves each year what proportion of one community will unite with the emigrants of another, so as to form a state of sufficient size; and the place for emigration is agreed upon at least a year before, and pioneers sent from each state to level rocks, and embank waters, and construct houses; so that when the emigrants at last go, they find a city already made, and a country around it at least partially cleared. Our hardy life as children make us take cheerfully to travel and adventure. I mean to emigrate myself when of age."

"Do the emigrants always select places hitherto uninhabited and barren?"

"As yet generally, because it is our rule never to destroy except when necessary to our well-being. Of course, we cannot settle in lands already occupied by the Vril-ya; and if we take the cultivated lands of the other races of Ana, we must utterly destroy the previous inhabitants. Sometimes, as it is, we take waste spots, and find that a troublesome, quarrelsome race of Ana, especially if under the administration of Koom-Posh or Glek-Nas, resents our vicinity, and picks a quarrel with us; then, of course, as menacing our welfare, we destroy it: there is no coming to terms of peace with a race so idiotic that it is always changing the form of government which represents it. Koom-Posh," said the child, emphatically, "is bad enough, still it has brains, though at the back of its head, and is not without a heart; but in Glek-Nas the brain and heart of the creatures disappear, and they become all jaws, claws, and belly." "You express yourself strongly. Allow me to inform you that I myself, and I am proud to say it, am the citizen of a Koom-Posh."

"I no longer," answered Taee, "wonder to see you here so far from your home. What was the condition of your native community before it became a Koom-Posh?"

"A settlement of emigrants—like those settlements which your tribe sends forth—but so far unlike your settlements, that it was dependent on the state from which it came. It shook off that yoke, and, crowned with eternal glory, became a Koom-Posh."

"Eternal glory! How long has the Koom-Posh lasted?"

"About 100 years."

"The length of an An's life—a very young community. In much less than another 100 years your Koom-Posh will be a Glek-Nas."

"Nay, the oldest states in the world I come from, have such faith in its duration, that they are all gradually shaping their institutions so as to melt into ours, and their most thoughtful politicians say that, whether they like it or not, the inevitable tendency of these old states is towards Koom-Posh-erie."

"The old states?"

"Yes, the old states."

"With populations very small in proportion to the area of productive land?"

"On the contrary, with populations very large in proportion to that area."

"I see! old states indeed!—so old as to become drivelling if they don't pack off that surplus population as we do ours—very old states!—very, very old! Pray, Tish, do you think it wise for very old men to try to turn head-over-heels as very young children do? And if you ask them why they attempted such antics, should you not laugh if they answered that by imitating very young children they could become very young children themselves? Ancient history abounds with instances of this sort a great many thousand years ago—and in every instance a very old state that played at Koom-Posh soon tumbled into Glek-Nas. Then, in horror of its own self, it cried out for a master, as an old man in his dotage cries out for a nurse; and after a succession of masters or nurses, more or less long, that very old state died out of history. A very old state attempting Koom-Posh-erie is like a very old man who pulls down the house to which he has been accustomed, but he has so exhausted his vigour in pulling down, that all he can do in the way of rebuilding is to run up a crazy hut, in which himself and his successors whine out, 'How the wind blows! How the walls shake!'"

"My dear Taee, I make all excuse for your unenlightened prejudices, which every schoolboy educated in a Koom-Posh could easily controvert, though he might not be so precociously learned in ancient history as you appear to be."

"I learned! not a bit of it. But would a schoolboy, educated in your Koom-Posh, ask his great-great-grandfather or great-great-grandmother to stand on his or her head with the feet uppermost? And if the poor old folks hesitated—say, 'What do you fear?—see how I do it!'"

"Taee, I disdain to argue with a child of your age. I repeat, I make allowances for your want of that culture which a Koom-Posh alone can bestow."

"I, in my turn," answered Taee, with an air of the suave but lofty good breeding which characterises his race, "not only make allowances for you as not educated among the Vril-ya, but I entreat you to vouchsafe me your pardon for the insufficient respect to the habits and opinions of so amiable a Tish!"

I ought before to have observed that I was commonly called Tish by my host and his family, as being a polite and indeed a pet name, literally signifying a small barbarian; the children apply it endearingly to the tame species of Frog which they keep in their gardens.

We had now reached the banks of a lake, and Taee here paused to point out to me the ravages made in fields skirting it. "The enemy certainly lies within these waters," said Taee. "Observe what shoals of fish are crowded together at the margin. Even the great fishes with the small ones, who are their habitual prey and who generally shun them, all forget their instincts in the presence of a common destroyer. This reptile certainly must belong to the class of Krek-a, which are more devouring than any other, and are said to be among the few surviving species of the world's dreadest inhabitants before the

Ana were created. The appetite of a Krek is insatiable—it feeds alike upon vegetable and animal life; but for the swift-footed creatures of the elk species it is too slow in its movements. Its favourite dainty is an An when it can catch him unawares; and hence the Ana destroy it relentlessly whenever it enters their dominion. I have heard that when our forefathers first cleared this country, these monsters, and others like them, abounded, and, vril being then undiscovered, many of our race were devoured. It was impossible to exterminate them wholly till that discovery which constitutes the power and sustains the civilisation of our race. But after the uses of vril became familiar to us, all creatures inimical to us were soon annihilated. Still, once a-year or so, one of these enormous creatures wanders from the unreclaimed and savage districts beyond, and within my memory one has seized upon a young Gy who was bathing in this very lake. Had she been on land and armed with her staff, it would not have dared even to show itself; for, like all savage creatures, the reptile has a marvellous instinct, which warns it against the bearer of the vril wand. How they teach their young to avoid him, though seen for the first time, is one of those mysteries which you may ask Zee to explain, for I cannot. The reptile in this instinct does but resemble our wild birds and animals, which will not come in reach of a man armed with a gun. When the electric wires were first put up, partridges struck against them in their flight, and fell down wounded. No younger generations of partridges meet with a similar accident. So long as I stand here, the monster will not stir from its lurking-place; but we must now decoy it forth."

"Will that not be difficult?"

"Not at all. Seat yourself yonder on that crag (about one hundred yards from the bank), while I retire to a distance. In a short time the reptile will catch sight or scent of you, and perceiving that you are no vril-bearer, will come forth to devour you. As soon as it is fairly out of the water, it becomes my prey."

"Do you mean to tell me that I am to be the decoy to that horrible monster which could engulf me within its jaws in a second! I beg to decline."

The child laughed. "Fear nothing," said he; "only sit still."

Instead of obeying the command, I made a bound, and was about to take fairly to my heels, when Taee touched me slightly on the shoulder, and, fixing his eyes steadily on mine, I was rooted to the spot. All power of volition left me. Submissive to the infant's gesture, I followed him to the crag he had indicated, and seated myself there in silence. Most readers have seen something of the effects of electro-biology, whether genuine or spurious. No professor of that doubtful craft had ever been able to influence a thought or a movement of mine, but I was a mere machine at the will of this terrible child. Meanwhile he expanded his wings, soared aloft, and alighted amidst a copse at the brow of a hill at some distance.

I was alone; and turning my eyes with an indescribable sensation of horror towards the lake, I kept them fixed on its water, spell-bound. It might be ten or fifteen minutes, to me it seemed ages, before the still surface, gleaming under the lamplight, began to be agitated towards the centre. At the same time the shoals of fish near the margin evinced their sense of the enemy's approach by splash and leap and bubbling circle. I could detect their hurried flight hither and thither, some even casting themselves ashore. A long, dark, undulous furrow came moving along the waters, nearer and nearer, till the vast head of the reptile emerged—its jaws bristling with fangs, and its dull eyes fixing themselves hungrily on the spot where I sat motionless. And now its fore feet were on the strand—now its enormous breast, scaled on either side as in armour, in the centre showing its corrugated skin of a dull venomous yellow; and now its whole length was on the land, a hundred feet or more from the jaw to the tail. Another stride of those ghastly feet would have brought it to the spot where I sat. There was but a moment between me and this grim form of death, when what seemed a flash of lightning shot through the air, smote, and, for a space of time briefer than that in which a man can draw his breath, enveloped the monster; and then, as the flash vanished, there lay before me a blackened, charred, smouldering mass, a something gigantic, but of which even the outlines of form were burned away, and rapidly crumbling into dust and ashes. I remained still seated, still speechless, ice-cold with a new sensation of dread; what had been horror was now awe.

I felt the child's hand on my head—fear left me—the spell was broken—I rose up. "You see with what ease the Vril-ya destroy their enemies," said Taee; and then, moving towards the bank, he contemplated the smouldering relics of the monster, and said quietly, "I have destroyed larger creatures, but none with so much pleasure. Yes, it IS a Krek; what suffering it must have inflicted while it lived!" Then he took up the poor fishes that had flung themselves ashore, and restored them mercifully to their native element.

Chapter XIX.

As we walked back to the town, Taee took a new and circuitous way, in order to show me what, to use a familiar term, I will call the 'Station,' from which emigrants or travellers to other communities commence their journeys. I had, on a former occasion, expressed a wish to see their vehicles. These I found to be of two kinds, one for land journeys, one for aerial voyages: the former were of all sizes and forms, some not larger than an ordinary carriage, some movable houses of one story and containing several rooms, furnished according to the ideas of comfort or luxury which are entertained by the Vril-ya. The aerial vehicles were of light substances, not the least resembling our balloons, but rather our boats and pleasure-vessels, with helm and rudder, with large wings or paddles, and a central machine worked by vril. All the vehicles both for land or air were indeed worked by that potent and mysterious agency.

I saw a convoy set out on its journey, but it had few passengers, containing chiefly articles of merchandise, and was bound to a neighbouring community; for among all the tribes of the Vril-ya there is considerable commercial interchange. I may here observe, that their money currency does not consist of the precious metals, which are too common among them for that purpose. The smaller coins in ordinary use are manufactured from a peculiar fossil shell, the comparatively scarce remnant of some very early deluge, or other convulsion of nature, by which a species has become extinct. It is minute, and flat as an oyster, and takes a jewel-like polish. This coinage circulates among all the tribes of the Vril-ya. Their larger transactions are carried on much like ours, by bills of exchange, and thin metallic plates which answer the purpose of our bank-notes.

Let me take this occasion of adding that the taxation among the tribe I became acquainted with was very considerable, compared with the amount of population. But I never heard that any one grumbled at it, for it was devoted to purposes of universal utility, and indeed necessary to the civilisation of the tribe. The cost of lighting so large a range of country, of providing for emigration, of maintaining the public buildings at which the various operations of national intellect were carried on, from the first education of an infant to the departments in which the College of Sages were perpetually trying new experiments in mechanical science; all these involved the necessity for considerable state funds. To these I must add an item that struck me as very singular. I have said that all the human labour required by the state is carried on by children up to the marriageable age. For this labour the state pays, and at a rate immeasurably higher than our own remuneration to labour even in the United States. According to their theory, every child, male or female, on attaining the marriageable age, and there terminating the period of labour, should have acquired enough for an independent competence during life. As, no matter what the disparity of fortune in the parents, all the children must equally serve, so all are equally paid according to their several ages or the nature of their work. Where the parents or friends choose to retain a child in their own service, they must pay into the public fund in the same ratio as the state pays to the children it employs; and this sum is handed over to the child when the period of service expires. This practice serves, no doubt, to render the notion of social equality familiar and agreeable; and if it may be said that all the children form a democracy, no less truly it may be said that all the adults form an aristocracy. The exquisite politeness and refinement of manners among the Vril-ya, the generosity of their sentiments, the absolute leisure they enjoy for following out their own private pursuits, the amenities of their domestic intercourse, in which they seem as members of one noble order that can have no distrust of each other's word or deed, all combine to make the Vril-ya the most perfect nobility which a political disciple of Plato or Sidney could conceive for the ideal of an aristocratic republic.

Chapter XX.

From the date of the expedition with Taee which I have just narrated, the child paid me frequent visits. He had taken a liking to me, which I cordially returned. Indeed, as he was not yet twelve years old, and had not commenced the course of scientific studies with which childhood closes in that country, my intellect was less inferior to his than to that of the elder members of his race, especially of the Gy-ei, and most especially of the accomplished Zee. The children of the Vril-ya, having upon their minds the weight of so many active duties and grave responsibilities, are not generally mirthful; but Taee, with all his wisdom, had much of the playful good-humour one often finds the characteristic of elderly men of genius. He felt that sort of pleasure in my society which a boy of a similar age in the upper world has in the company of a pet dog or monkey. It amused him to try and teach me the ways of his people, as it amuses a nephew of mine to make his poodle walk on his hind legs or jump through a hoop. I willingly lent myself to such experiments, but I never achieved the success of the poodle. I was very much interested at first in the attempt to ply the wings which the youngest of the Vril-ya use as nimbly and easily as ours do their legs and arms; but my efforts were attended with contusions serious enough to make me abandon them in despair.

These wings, as I before said, are very large, reaching to the knee, and in repose thrown back so as to form a very graceful mantle. They are composed from the feathers of a gigantic bird that abounds in the rocky heights of the country—the colour mostly white, but sometimes with reddish streaks. They are fastened round the shoulders with light but strong springs of steel; and, when expanded, the arms slide through loops for that purpose, forming, as it were, a stout central membrane. As the arms are raised, a tubular lining beneath the vest or tunic becomes, by mechanical contrivance inflated with air, increased or diminished at will by the movement of the arms, and serving to buoy the whole form as on bladders. The wings and the balloon-like apparatus are highly charged with vril; and when the body is thus wafted upward, it seems to become singularly lightened of its weight. I found it easy enough to soar from the ground; indeed, when the wings were spread it was scarcely possible not to soar, but then came the difficulty and the danger. I utterly failed in the power to use and direct the pinions, though I am considered among my own race unusually alert and ready in bodily exercises, and am a very practiced swimmer. I could only make the most confused and blundering efforts at flight. I was the servant of the wings; the wings were not my servants—they were beyond my control; and when by a violent strain of muscle, and, I must fairly own, in that abnormal strength which is given by excessive fright, I curbed their gyrations and brought them near to the body, it seemed as if I lost the sustaining power stored in them and the connecting bladders, as when the air is let out of a balloon, and found myself precipitated again to the earth; saved, indeed, by some spasmodic flutterings, from being dashed to pieces, but not saved from the bruises and the stun of a heavy fall. I would, however, have persevered in my attempts, but for the advice or the commands of the scientific Zee, who had benevolently accompanied my flutterings, and, indeed, on the last occasion, flying just under me, received my form as it fell on her own expanded wings, and preserved me from breaking my head on the roof of the pyramid from which we had ascended.

"I see," she said, "that your trials are in vain, not from the fault of the wings and their appurtenances, nor from any imperfectness and malformation of your own corpuscular system, but from irremediable, because organic, defect in your power of volition. Learn that the connection between the will and the agencies of that fluid which has been subjected to the control of the Vril-ya was never established by the first discoverers, never achieved by a single generation; it has gone on increasing, like other properties of race, in proportion as it has been uniformly transmitted from parent to child, so that, at last, it has become an instinct; and an infant An of our race wills to fly as intuitively and unconsciously as he wills to walk. He thus plies his invented or artificial wings with as much safety as a bird plies those with which it is born. I did not think sufficiently of this when I allowed you to try an experiment which allured me, for I have longed to have in you a companion. I shall abandon the experiment now. Your life is becoming dear to me." Herewith the Gy's voice and face softened, and I felt more seriously alarmed than I had been in my previous flights.

Now that I am on the subject of wings, I ought not to omit mention of a custom among the Gy-ei which seems to me very pretty and tender in the sentiment it implies. A Gy wears wings habitually when yet a virgin—she joins the Ana in their aerial sports—she adventures alone and afar into the wilder regions of the sunless world: in the boldness and height of her soarings, not less than in the grace of her movements, she excels the opposite sex. But, from the day of her marriage she wears wings no more, she suspends them with her own willing hand over the nuptial couch, never to be resumed unless the marriage tie be severed by divorce or death.

Now when Zee's voice and eyes thus softened—and at that softening I prophetically recoiled and shuddered—Taee, who had accompanied us in our flights, but who, child-like, had been much more amused with my awkwardness, than sympathising in my fears or aware of my danger, hovered over us, poised amidst spread wings, and hearing the endearing words of the young Gy, laughed aloud. Said he, "If the Tish cannot learn the use of wings, you may still be his companion, Zee, for you can suspend your own."

Chapter XXI.

I had for some time observed in my host's highly informed and powerfully proportioned daughter that kindly and protective sentiment which, whether above the earth or below it, an all-wise Providence has bestowed upon the feminine division of the human race. But until very lately I had ascribed it to that affection for 'pets' which a human female at every age shares with a human child. I now became painfully aware that the feeling with which Zee deigned to regard me was different from that which I had inspired in Taee. But this conviction gave me none of that complacent gratification which the vanity of man ordinarily conceives from a flattering appreciation of his personal merits on the part of the fair sex; on the contrary, it inspired me with fear. Yet of all the Gy-ei in the community, if Zee were perhaps the wisest and the strongest, she was, by common repute, the gentlest, and she was certainly the most popularly beloved. The desire to aid, to succour, to protect, to comfort, to bless, seemed to pervade her whole being. Though the complicated miseries that originate in penury and guilt are unknown to the social system of the Vril-ya, still, no sage had yet discovered in vril an agency which could banish sorrow from life; and wherever amongst her people sorrow found its way, there Zee followed in the mission of comforter. Did some sister Gy fail to secure the love she sighed for? Zee sought her out, and brought all the resources of her lore, and all the consolations of her sympathy, to bear upon a grief that so needs the solace of a confidant. In the rare cases, when grave illness seized upon childhood or youth, and the cases, less rare, when, in the hardy and adventurous probation of infants, some accident, attended with pain and injury occurred, Zee forsook her studies and her sports, and became the healer and nurse. Her favourite flights were towards the extreme boundaries of the domain where children were stationed on guard against outbreaks of warring forces in nature, or the invasions of devouring animals, so that she might warn them of any peril which her knowledge detected or foresaw, or be at hand if any harm had befallen. Nay, even in the exercise of her scientific acquirements there was a concurrent benevolence of purpose and will. Did she learn any novelty in invention that would be useful to the practitioner of some special art or craft? she hastened to communicate and explain it. Was some veteran sage of the College perplexed and wearied with the toil of an abstruse study? she would patiently devote herself to his aid, work out details for him, sustain his spirits with her hopeful smile, quicken his wit with her luminous suggestion, be to him, as it were, his own good genius made visible as the strengthener and inspirer. The same tenderness she exhibited to the inferior creatures. I have often known her bring home some sick and wounded animal, and tend and cherish it as a mother would tend and cherish her stricken child. Many a time when I sat in the balcony, or hanging garden, on which my window opened, I have watched her rising in the air on her radiant wings, and in a few moments groups of infants below, catching sight of her, would soar upward with joyous sounds of greeting; clustering and sporting around her, so that she seemed a very centre of innocent delight. When I have walked with her amidst the rocks and valleys without the city, the elk-deer would scent or see her from afar, come bounding up, eager for the caress of her hand, or follow her footsteps, till dismissed by some musical whisper that the creature had learned to comprehend. It is the fashion among the virgin Gy-ei to wear on their foreheads a circlet, or coronet, with gems resembling opals, arranged in four points or rays like stars. These are lustreless in ordinary use, but if touched by the vril wand they take a clear lambent flame, which illuminates, yet not burns. This serves as an ornament in their festivities, and as a lamp, if, in their wanderings beyond their artificial lights, they have to traverse the dark. There are times, when I have seen Zee's thoughtful majesty of face lighted up by this crowning halo, that I could scarcely believe her to be a creature of mortal birth, and bent my head before her as the vision of a being among the celestial orders. But never once did my heart feel for this lofty type of the noblest womanhood a sentiment of human love. Is it that, among the race I belong to, man's pride so far influences his passions that woman loses to him her special charm of woman if he feels her to be in all things eminently superior to himself? But by what strange infatuation could this peerless daughter of a race which, in the supremacy of its powers and the felicity of its conditions, ranked all other races in the category of barbarians, have deigned to honour me with her preference? In personal qualifications, though I passed for good-looking amongst the people I came from, the handsomest of my countrymen might have seemed insignificant and homely beside the grand and serene type of beauty which characterised the aspect of the Vril-ya.

That novelty, the very difference between myself and those to whom Zee was accustomed, might serve to bias her fancy was probable enough, and as the reader will see later, such a cause might suffice to account for the predilection with which I was distinguished by a young Gy scarcely out of her childhood, and very inferior in all respects to Zee. But whoever will consider those tender characteristics which I have just ascribed to the daughter of Aph-Lin, may readily conceive that the main cause of my attraction to her was in her instinctive desire to cherish, to comfort, to protect, and, in protecting, to sustain and to exalt. Thus, when I look back, I account for the only weakness unworthy of her lofty nature, which bowed the daughter of the Vril-ya to a woman's affection for one so inferior to herself as was her father's guest. But be the cause what it may, the consciousness that I had inspired such affection thrilled me with awe—a moral awe of her very imperfections, of her mysterious powers, of the inseparable distinctions between her race and my own; and with that awe, I must confess to my shame, there combined the more material and ignoble dread of the perils to which her preference would expose me.

Under these anxious circumstances, fortunately, my conscience and sense of honour were free from reproach. It became clearly my duty, if Zee's preference continued manifest, to intimate it to my host, with, of course, all the delicacy which is ever to be preserved by a well-bred man in confiding to another any degree of favour by which one of the fair sex may condescend to distinguish him. Thus, at all events, I should be freed from responsibility or suspicion of voluntary participation in the sentiments of Zee; and the superior wisdom of my host might probably suggest some sage extrication from my perilous dilemma. In this resolve I obeyed the ordinary instinct of civilised and moral man, who, erring though he be, still generally prefers the right course in those cases where it is obviously against his inclinations, his interests, and his safety to elect the wrong one.

Chapter XXII.

As the reader has seen, Aph-Lin had not favoured my general and unrestricted intercourse with his countrywomen. Though relying on my promise to abstain from giving any information as to the world I had left, and still more on the promise of those to whom had been put the same request, not to question me, which Zee had exacted from Taee, yet he did not feel sure that, if I were allowed to mix with the strangers whose curiosity the sight of me had aroused, I could sufficiently guard myself against their inquiries. When I went out, therefore, it was never alone; I was always accompanied either by one of my host's family, or my child-friend Taee. Bra, Aph-Lin's wife, seldom stirred beyond the gardens which surrounded the house, and was fond of reading the ancient literature, which contained something of romance and adventure not to be found in the writings of recent ages, and presented pictures of a life unfamiliar to her experience and interesting to her imagination; pictures, indeed, of a life more resembling that which we lead every day above ground, coloured by our sorrows, sins, passions, and much to her what the tales of the Genii or the Arabian Nights are to us. But her love of reading did not prevent Bra from the discharge of her duties as mistress of the largest household in the city. She went daily the round of the chambers, and saw that the automata and other mechanical contrivances were in order, that the numerous children employed by Aph-Lin, whether in his private or public capacity, were carefully tended. Bra also inspected the accounts of the whole estate, and it was her great delight to assist her husband in the business connected with his office as chief administrator of the Lighting Department, so that her avocations necessarily kept her much within doors. The two sons were both completing their education at the College of Sages; and the elder, who had a strong passion for mechanics, and especially for works connected with the machinery of timepieces and automata, had decided on devoting himself to these pursuits, and was now occupied in constructing a shop or warehouse, at which his inventions could be exhibited and sold. The younger son preferred farming and rural occupations; and when not attending the College, at which he chiefly studied the theories of agriculture, was much absorbed by his practical application of that science to his father's lands. It will be seen by this how completely equality of ranks is established among this people—a shopkeeper being of exactly the same grade in estimation as the large landed proprietor. Aph-Lin was the wealthiest member of the community, and his eldest son preferred keeping a shop to any other avocation; nor was this choice thought to show any want of elevated notions on his part.

This young man had been much interested in examining my watch, the works of which were new to him, and was greatly pleased when I made him a present of it. Shortly after, he returned the gift with interest, by a watch of his own construction, marking both the time as in my watch and the time as kept among the Vril-ya. I have that watch still, and it has been much admired by many among the most eminent watchmakers of London and Paris. It is of gold, with diamond hands and figures, and it plays a favorite tune among the Vril-ya in striking the hours: it only requires to be wound up once in ten months, and has never gone wrong since I had it. These young brothers being thus occupied, my usual companions in that family, when I went abroad, were my host or his daughter. Now, agreeably with the honourable conclusions I had come to, I began to excuse myself from Zee's invitations to go out alone with her, and seized an occasion when that learned Gy was delivering a lecture at the College of Sages to ask Aph-Lin to show me his country-seat. As this was at some little distance, and as Aph-Lin was not fond of walking, while I had discreetly relinquished all attempts at flying, we proceeded to our destination in one of the aerial boats belonging to my host. A child of eight years old, in his employ, was our conductor. My host and myself reclined on cushions, and I found the movement very easy and luxurious. "Aph-Lin," said I, "you will not, I trust, be displeased with me, if I ask your permission to travel for a short time, and visit other tribes or communities of your illustrious race. I have also a strong desire to see those nations which do not adopt your institutions, and which you consider as savages. It would interest me greatly to notice what are the distinctions between them and the races whom we consider civilised in the world I have left."

"It is utterly impossible that you should go hence alone," said Aph-Lin. "Even among the Vril-ya you would be exposed to great dangers. Certain peculiarities of formation and colour, and the extraordinary phenomenon of hirsute bushes upon your cheeks and chin, denoting in you a species of An distinct alike from our own race and any known race of barbarians yet extant, would attract, of course, the special attention of the College of Sages in whatever community of Vril-ya you visited, and it would depend upon the individual temper of some individual sage whether you would be received, as you have been here, hospitably, or whether you would not be at once dissected for scientific purposes. Know that when the Tur first took you to his house, and while you were there put to sleep by Taee in order to recover from your previous pain or fatigue, the sages summoned by the Tur were divided in opinion whether you were a harmless or an obnoxious animal. During your unconscious state your teeth were examined, and they clearly showed that you were not only graminivorous but carnivorous. Carnivorous animals of your size are always destroyed, as being of savage and dangerous nature. Our teeth, as you have doubtless observed,* are not those of the creatures who devour flesh."

* I never had observed it; and, if I had, am not physiologist enough to have distinguished the difference.

"It is, indeed, maintained by Zee and other philosophers, that as, in remote ages, the Ana did prey upon living beings of the brute species, their teeth must have been fitted for that purpose. But, even if so, they have been modified by hereditary transmission, and suited to the food on which we now exist; nor are even the barbarians, who adopt the turbulent and ferocious institutions of Glek-Nas, devourers of flesh like beasts of prey.

"In the course of this dispute it was proposed to dissect you; but Taee begged you off, and the Tur being, by office, averse to all novel experiments at variance with our custom of sparing life, except where it is clearly proved to be for the good of the community to take it, sent to me, whose business it is, as the richest man of the state, to afford hospitality to strangers from a distance. It was at my option to decide whether or not you were a stranger whom I could safely admit. Had I declined to receive you, you would have been handed over to the College of Sages, and what might there have befallen you I do not like to conjecture. Apart from this danger, you might chance to encounter some child of four years old, just put in possession of his vril staff; and who, in alarm at your strange appearance, and in the impulse of the moment, might reduce you to a cinder. Taee himself was about to do so when he first saw you, had his father not checked his hand. Therefore I say you cannot travel alone, but with Zee you would be safe; and I have no doubt that she would accompany you on a tour round the neighbouring communities of Vril-ya (to the savage states, No!): I will ask her."

Now, as my main object in proposing to travel was to escape from Zee, I hastily exclaimed, "Nay, pray do not! I relinquish my design. You have said enough as to its dangers to deter me from it; and I can scarcely think it right that a young Gy of the personal attractions of your lovely daughter should travel into other regions without a better protector than a Tish of my insignificant strength and stature."

Aph-Lin emitted the soft sibilant sound which is the nearest approach to laughter that a full-grown An permits to himself, ere he replied: "Pardon my discourteous but momentary indulgence of mirth at any observation seriously made by my guest. I could not but be amused at the idea of Zee, who is so fond of protecting others that children call her 'THE GUARDIAN,' needing a protector herself against any dangers arising from the audacious admiration of males. Know that our Gy-ei, while unmarried, are accustomed to travel alone among other tribes, to see if they find there some An who may please them more than the Ana they find at home. Zee has already made three such journeys, but hitherto her heart has been untouched."

Here the opportunity which I sought was afforded to me, and I said, looking down, and with faltering voice, "Will you, my kind host, promise to pardon me, if what I am about to say gives offence?"

"Say only the truth, and I cannot be offended; or, could I be so, it would not be for me, but for you to pardon."

"Well, then, assist me to quit you, and, much as I should have like to witness more of the wonders, and enjoy more of the felicity, which belong to your people, let me return to my own."

"I fear there are reasons why I cannot do that; at all events, not without permission of the Tur, and he, probably, would not grant it. You are not destitute of intelligence; you may (though I do not think so) have concealed the degree of destructive powers possessed by your people; you might, in short, bring upon us some danger; and if the Tur entertains that idea, it would clearly be his duty, either to put an end to you, or enclose you in a cage for the rest of your existence. But why should you wish to leave a state of society which you so politely allow to be more felicitous than your own?"

"Oh, Aph-Lin! My answer is plain. Lest in naught, and unwittingly, I should betray your hospitality; lest, in the caprice of will which in our world is proverbial among the other sex, and from which even a Gy is not free, your adorable daughter should deign to regard me, though a Tish, as if I were a civilised An, and—and—and—-" "Court you as her spouse," put in Aph-Lin, gravely, and without any visible sign of surprise or displeasure.

"You have said it."

"That would be a misfortune," resumed my host, after a pause, "and I feel you have acted as you ought in warning me. It is, as you imply, not uncommon for an unwedded Gy to conceive tastes as to the object she covets which appear whimsical to others; but there is no power to compel a young Gy to any course opposed to that which she chooses to pursue. All we can to is to reason with her, and experience tells us that the whole College of Sages would find it vain to reason with a Gy in a matter that concerns her choice in love. I grieve for you, because such a marriage would be against the A-glauran, or good of the community, for the children of such a marriage would adulterate the race: they might even come into the world with the teeth of carnivorous animals; this could not be allowed: Zee, as a Gy, cannot be controlled; but you, as a Tish, can be destroyed. I advise you, then, to resist her addresses; to tell her plainly that you can never return her love. This happens constantly. Many an An, however, ardently wooed by one Gy, rejects her, and puts an end to her persecution by wedding another. The same course is open to you."

"No; for I cannot wed another Gy without equally injuring the community, and exposing it to the chance of rearing carnivorous children."

"That is true. All I can say, and I say it with the tenderness due to a Tish, and the respect due to a guest, is frankly this—if you yield, you will become a cinder. I must leave it to you to take the best way you can to defend yourself. Perhaps you had better tell Zee that she is ugly. That assurance on the lips of him she woos generally suffices to chill the most ardent Gy. Here we are at my country-house."

Chapter XXIII.

I confess that my conversation with Aph-Lin, and the extreme coolness with which he stated his inability to control the dangerous caprice of his daughter, and treated the idea of the reduction into a cinder to which her amorous flame might expose my too seductive person, took away the pleasure I should otherwise have had in the contemplation of my host's country-seat, and the astonishing perfection of the machinery by which his farming operations were conducted. The house differed in appearance from the massive and sombre building which Aph-Lin inhabited in the city, and which seemed akin to the rocks out of which the city itself had been hewn into shape. The walls of the country-seat were composed by trees placed a few feet apart from each other, the interstices being filled in with the transparent metallic substance which serves the purpose of glass among the Ana. These trees were all in flower, and the effect was very pleasing, if not in the best taste. We were received at the porch by life-like automata, who conducted us into a chamber, the like to which I never saw before, but have often on summer days dreamily imagined. It was a bower—half room, half garden. The walls were one mass of climbing flowers. The open spaces, which we call windows, and in which, here, the metallic surfaces were slided back, commanded various views; some, of the wide landscape with its lakes and rocks; some, of small limited expanses answering to our conservatories, filled with tiers of flowers. Along the sides of the room were flower-beds, interspersed with cushions for repose. In the centre of the floor was a cistern and a fountain of that liquid light which I have presumed to be naphtha. It was luminous and of a roseate hue; it sufficed without lamps to light up the room with a subdued radiance. All around the fountain was carpeted with a soft deep lichen, not green (I have never seen that colour in the vegetation of this country), but a quiet brown, on which the eye reposes with the same sense of relief as that with which in the upper world it reposes on green. In the outlets upon flowers (which I have compared to our conservatories) there were singing birds innumerable, which, while we remained in the room, sang in those harmonies of tune to which they are, in these parts, so wonderfully trained. The roof was open. The whole scene had charms for every sense—music form the birds, fragrance from the flowers, and varied beauty to the eye at every aspect. About all was a voluptuous repose. What a place, methought, for a honeymoon, if a Gy bride were a little less formidably armed not only with the rights of woman, but with the powers of man! But when one thinks of a Gy, so learned, so tall, so stately, so much above the standard of the creature we call woman as was Zee, no! even if I had felt no fear of being reduced to a cinder, it is not of her I should have dreamed in that bower so constructed for dreams of poetic love.

The automata reappeared, serving one of those delicious liquids which form the innocent wines of the Vril-ya.

"Truly," said I, "this is a charming residence, and I can scarcely conceive why you do not settle yourself here instead of amid the gloomier abodes of the city."

"As responsible to the community for the administration of light, I am compelled to reside chiefly in the city, and can only come hither for short intervals."

"But since I understand from you that no honours are attached to your office, and it involves some trouble, why do you accept it?"

"Each of us obeys without question the command of the Tur. He said, 'Be it requested that Aph-Lin shall be the Commissioner of Light,' so I had no choice; but having held the office now for a long time, the cares, which were at first unwelcome, have become, if not pleasing, at least endurable. We are all formed by custom—even the difference of our race from the savage is but the transmitted continuance of custom, which becomes, through hereditary descent, part and parcel of our nature. You see there are Ana who even reconcile themselves to the responsibilities of chief magistrate, but no one would do so if his duties had not been rendered so light, or if there were any questions as to compliance with his requests."

"Not even if you thought the requests unwise or unjust?"

"We do not allow ourselves to think so, and, indeed, everything goes on as if each and all governed themselves according to immemorial custom."

"When the chief magistrate dies or retires, how do you provide for his successor?"

"The An who has discharged the duties of chief magistrate for many years is the best person to choose one by whom those duties may be understood, and he generally names his successor."

"His son, perhaps?"

"Seldom that; for it is not an office any one desires or seeks, and a father naturally hesitates to constrain his son. But if the Tur himself decline to make a choice, for fear it might be supposed that he owed some grudge to the person on whom his choice would settle, then there are three of the College of Sages who draw lots among themselves which shall have the power to elect the chief. We consider that the judgment of one An of ordinary capacity is better than the judgment of three or more, however wise they may be; for among three there would probably be disputes, and where there are disputes, passion clouds judgment. The worst choice made by one who has no motive in choosing wrong, is better than the best choice made by many who have many motives for not choosing right."

"You reverse in your policy the maxims adopted in my country."

"Are you all, in your country, satisfied with your governors?"

"All! Certainly not; the governors that most please some are sure to be those most displeasing to others."

"Then our system is better than yours." "For you it may be; but according to our system a Tish could not be reduced to a cinder if a female compelled him to marry her; and as a Tish I sigh to return to my native world."

"Take courage, my dear little guest; Zee can't compel you to marry her. She can only entice you to do so. Don't be enticed. Come and look round my domain."

We went forth into a close, bordered with sheds; for though the Ana keep no stock for food, there are some animals which they rear for milking and others for shearing. The former have no resemblance to our cows, nor the latter to our sheep, nor do I believe such species exist amongst them. They use the milk of three varieties of animal: one resembles the antelope, but is much larger, being as tall as a camel; the other two are smaller, and, though differing somewhat from each other, resemble no creature I ever saw on earth. They are very sleek and of rounded proportions; their colour that of the dappled deer, with very mild countenances and beautiful dark eyes. The milk of these three creatures differs in richness and taste. It is usually diluted with water, and flavoured with the juice of a peculiar and perfumed fruit, and in itself is very nutritious and palatable. The animal whose fleece serves them for clothing and many other purposes, is more like the Italian she-goat than any other creature, but is considerably larger, has no horns, and is free from the displeasing odour of our goats. Its fleece is not thick, but very long and fine; it varies in colour, but is never white, more generally of a slate-like or lavender hue. For clothing it is usually worn dyed to suit the taste of the wearer. These animals were exceedingly tame, and were treated with extraordinary care and affection by the children (chiefly female) who tended them.

We then went through vast storehouses filled with grains and fruits. I may here observe that the main staple of food among these people consists—firstly, of a kind of corn much larger in ear than our wheat, and which by culture is perpetually being brought into new varieties of flavour; and, secondly, of a fruit of about the size of a small orange, which, when gathered, is hard and bitter. It is stowed away for many months in their warehouses, and then becomes succulent and tender. Its juice, which is of dark-red colour, enters into most of their sauces. They have many kinds of fruit of the nature of the olive, from which delicious oils are extracted. They have a plant somewhat resembling the sugar-cane, but its juices are less sweet and of a delicate perfume. They have no bees nor honey-making insects, but they make much use of a sweet gum that oozes from a coniferous plant, not unlike the araucaria. Their soil teems also with esculent roots and vegetables, which it is the aim of their culture to improve and vary to the utmost. And I never remember any meal among this people, however it might be confined to the family household, in which some delicate novelty in such articles of food was not introduced. In fine, as I before observed, their cookery is exquisite, so diversified and nutritious that one does not miss animal food; and their own physical forms suffice to show that with them, at least, meat is not required for superior production of muscular fibre. They have no grapes—the drinks extracted from their fruits are innocent and refreshing. Their staple beverage, however, is water, in the choice of which they are very fastidious, distinguishing at once the slightest impurity.

"My younger son takes great pleasure in augmenting our produce," said Aph-Lin as we passed through the storehouses, "and therefore will inherit these lands, which constitute the chief part of my wealth. To my elder son such inheritance would be a great trouble and affliction."

"Are there many sons among you who think the inheritance of vast wealth would be a great trouble and affliction?"

"Certainly; there are indeed very few of the Vril-ya who do not consider that a fortune much above the average is a heavy burden. We are rather a lazy people after the age of childhood, and do not like undergoing more cares than we can help, and great wealth does give its owner many cares. For instance, it marks us out for public offices, which none of us like and none of us can refuse. It necessitates our taking a continued interest in the affairs of any of our poorer countrymen, so that we may anticipate their wants and see that none fall into poverty. There is an old proverb amongst us which says, 'The poor man's need is the rich man's shame—-'"

"Pardon me, if I interrupt you for a moment. You allow that some, even of the Vril-ya, know want, and need relief."

"If by want you mean the destitution that prevails in a Koom-Posh, THAT is impossible with us, unless an An has, by some extraordinary process, got rid of all his means, cannot or will not emigrate, and has either tired out the affectionate aid of this relations or personal friends, or refuses to accept it."

"Well, then, does he not supply the place of an infant or automaton, and become a labourer—a servant?"

"No; then we regard him as an unfortunate person of unsound reason, and place him, at the expense of the State, in a public building, where every comfort and every luxury that can mitigate his affliction are lavished upon him. But an An does not like to be considered out of his mind, and therefore such cases occur so seldom that the public building I speak of is now a deserted ruin, and the last inmate of it was an An whom I recollect to have seen in my childhood. He did not seem conscious of loss of reason, and wrote glaubs (poetry). When I spoke of wants, I meant such wants as an An with desires larger than his means sometimes entertains—for expensive singing-birds, or bigger houses, or country-gardens; and the obvious way to satisfy such wants is to buy of him something that he sells. Hence Ana like myself, who are very rich, are obliged to buy a great many things they do not require, and live on a very large scale where they might prefer to live on a small one. For instance, the great size of my house in the town is a source of much trouble to my wife, and even to myself; but I am compelled to have it thus incommodiously large, because, as the richest An of the community, I am appointed to entertain the strangers from the other communities when they visit us, which they do in great crowds twice-a-year, when certain periodical entertainments are held, and when relations scattered throughout all the realms of the Vril-ya joyfully reunite for a time. This hospitality, on a scale so extensive, is not to my taste, and therefore I should have been happier had I been less rich. But we must all bear the lot assigned to us in this short passage through time that we call life. After all, what are a hundred years, more or less, to the ages through which we must pass hereafter? Luckily, I have one son who likes great wealth. It is a rare exception to the general rule, and I own I cannot myself understand it."

After this conversation I sought to return to the subject which continued to weigh on my heart—viz., the chances of escape from Zee. But my host politely declined to renew that topic, and summoned our air-boat. On our way back we were met by Zee, who, having found us gone, on her return from the College of Sages, had unfurled her wings and flown in search of us.

Her grand, but to me unalluring, countenance brightened as she beheld me, and, poising herself beside the boat on her large outspread plumes, she said reproachfully to Aph-Lin—"Oh, father, was it right in you to hazard the life of your guest in a vehicle to which he is so unaccustomed? He might, by an incautious movement, fall over the side; and alas; he is not like us, he has no wings. It were death to him to fall. Dear one!" (she added, accosting my shrinking self in a softer voice), "have you no thought of me, that you should thus hazard a life which has become almost a part of mine? Never again be thus rash, unless I am thy companion. What terror thou hast stricken into me!"

I glanced furtively at Aph-Lin, expecting, at least, that he would indignantly reprove his daughter for expressions of anxiety and affection, which, under all the circumstances, would, in the world above ground, be considered immodest in the lips of a young female, addressed to a male not affianced to her, even if of the same rank as herself.

But so confirmed are the rights of females in that region, and so absolutely foremost among those rights do females claim the privilege of courtship, that Aph-Lin would no more have thought of reproving his virgin daughter than he would have thought of disobeying the orders of the Tur. In that country, custom, as he implied, is all in all.

He answered mildly, "Zee, the Tish is in no danger and it is my belief the he can take very good care of himself."

"I would rather that he let me charge myself with his care. Oh, heart of my heart, it was in the thought of thy danger that I first felt how much I loved thee!"

Never did man feel in such a false position as I did. These words were spoken loud in the hearing of Zee's father—in the hearing of the child who steered. I blushed with shame for them, and for her, and could not help replying angrily: "Zee, either you mock me, which, as your father's guest, misbecomes you, or the words you utter are improper for a maiden Gy to address even to an An of her own race, if he has not wooed her with the consent of her parents. How much more improper to address them to a Tish, who has never presumed to solicit your affections, and who can never regard you with other sentiments than those of reverence and awe!"

Aph-Lin made me a covert sing of approbation, but said nothing. "Be not so cruel!" exclaimed Zee, still in sonorous accents. "Can love command itself where it is truly felt? Do you suppose that a maiden Gy will conceal a sentiment that it elevates her to feel? What a country you must have come from!"

Here Aph-Lin gently interposed, saying, "Among the Tish-a the rights of your sex do not appear to be established, and at all events my guest may converse with you more freely if unchecked by the presence of others."

To this remark Zee made no reply, but, darting on me a tender reproachful glance, agitated her wings and fled homeward.

"I had counted, at least, on some aid from my host," I said bitterly, "in the perils to which his own daughter exposes me."

"I gave you the best aid I could. To contradict a Gy in her love affairs is to confirm her purpose. She allows no counsel to come between her and her affections."

Chapter XXIV.

On alighting from the air-boat, a child accosted Aph-Lin in the hall with a request that he would be present at the funeral obsequies of a relation who had recently departed from that nether world.

Now, I had never seen a burial-place or cemetery amongst this people, and, glad to seize even so melancholy an occasion to defer an encounter with Zee, I asked Aph-Lin if I might be permitted to witness with him the interment of his relation; unless, indeed, it were regarded as one of those sacred ceremonies to which a stranger to their race might not be admitted.

"The departure of an An to a happier world," answered my host, "when, as in the case of my kinsman, he has lived so long in this as to have lost pleasure in it, is rather a cheerful though quiet festival than a sacred ceremony, and you may accompany me if you will."

Preceded by the child-messenger, we walked up the main street to a house at some little distance, and, entering the hall, were conducted to a room on the ground floor, where we found several persons assembled round a couch on which was laid the deceased. It was an old man, who had, as I was told, lived beyond his 130th year. To judge by the calm smile on his countenance, he had passed away without suffering. One of the sons, who was now the head of the family, and who seemed in vigorous middle life, though he was considerably more than seventy, stepped forward with a cheerful face and told Aph-Lin "that the day before he died his father had seen in a dream his departed Gy, and was eager to be reunited to her, and restored to youth beneath the nearer smile of the All-Good."

While these two were talking, my attention was drawn to a dark metallic substance at the farther end of the room. It was about twenty feet in length, narrow in proportion, and all closed round, save, near the roof, there were small round holes through which might be seen a red light. From the interior emanated a rich and sweet perfume; and while I was conjecturing what purpose this machine was to serve, all the time-pieces in the town struck the hour with their solemn musical chime; and as that sound ceased, music of a more joyous character, but still of a joy subdued and tranquil, rang throughout the chamber, and from the walls beyond, in a choral peal. Symphonious with the melody, those in the room lifted their voices in chant. The words of this hymn were simple. They expressed no regret, no farewell, but rather a greeting to the new world whither the deceased had preceded the living. Indeed, in their language, the funeral hymn is called the 'Birth Song.' Then the corpse, covered by a long cerement, was tenderly lifted up by six of the nearest kinfolk and borne towards the dark thing I have described. I pressed forward to see what happened. A sliding door or panel at one end was lifted up—the body deposited within, on a shelf—the door reclosed—a spring a the side touched—a sudden 'whishing,' sighing sound heard from within; and lo! at the other end of the machine the lid fell down, and a small handful of smouldering dust dropped into a 'patera' placed to receive it. The son took up the 'patera' and said (in what I understood afterwards was the usual form of words), "Behold how great is the Maker! To this little dust He gave form and life and soul. It needs not this little dust for Him to renew form and life and soul to the beloved one we shall soon see again."

Each present bowed his head and pressed his hand to his heart. Then a young female child opened a small door within the wall, and I perceived, in the recess, shelves on which were placed many 'paterae' like that which the son held, save that they all had covers. With such a cover a Gy now approached the son, and placed it over the cup, on which it closed with a spring. On the lid were engraven the name of the deceased, and these words:—"Lent to us" (here the date of birth). "Recalled from us" (here the date of death).

The closed door shut with a musical sound, and all was over.

Chapter XXV.

"And this," said I, with my mind full of what I had witnessed—"this, I presume, is your usual form of burial?"

"Our invariable form," answered Aph-Lin. "What is it amongst your people?"

"We inter the body whole within the earth."

"What! To degrade the form you have loved and honoured, the wife on whose breast you have slept, to the loathsomeness of corruption?" "But if the soul lives again, can it matter whether the body waste within the earth or is reduced by that awful mechanism, worked, no doubt by the agency of vril, into a pinch of dust?"

"You answer well," said my host, "and there is no arguing on a matter of feeling; but to me your custom is horrible and repulsive, and would serve to invest death with gloomy and hideous associations. It is something, too, to my mind, to be able to preserve the token of what has been our kinsman or friend within the abode in which we live. We thus feel more sensibly that he still lives, though not visibly so to us. But our sentiments in this, as in all things, are created by custom. Custom is not to be changed by a wise An, any more than it is changed by a wise Community, without the greatest deliberation, followed by the most earnest conviction. It is only thus that change ceases to be changeability, and once made is made for good."

When we regained the house, Aph-Lin summoned some of the children in his service and sent them round to several of his friends, requesting their attendance that day, during the Easy Hours, to a festival in honour of his kinsman's recall to the All-Good. This was the largest and gayest assembly I ever witnessed during my stay among the Ana, and was prolonged far into the Silent Hours.

The banquet was spread in a vast chamber reserved especially for grand occasions. This differed from our entertainments, and was not without a certain resemblance to those we read of in the luxurious age of the Roman empire. There was not one great table set out, but numerous small tables, each appropriated to eight guests. It is considered that beyond that number conversation languishes and friendship cools. The Ana never laugh loud, as I have before observed, but the cheerful ring of their voices at the various tables betokened gaiety of intercourse. As they have no stimulant drinks, and are temperate in food, though so choice and dainty, the banquet itself did not last long. The tables sank through the floor, and then came musical entertainments for those who liked them. Many, however, wandered away:—some of the younger ascended in their wings, for the hall was roofless, forming aerial dances; others strolled through the various apartments, examining the curiosities with which they were stored, or formed themselves into groups for various games, the favourite of which is a complicated kind of chess played by eight persons. I mixed with the crowd, but was prevented joining in the conversation by the constant companionship of one or the other of my host's sons, appointed to keep me from obtrusive questionings. The guests, however, noticed me but slightly; they had grown accustomed to my appearance, seeing me so often in the streets, and I had ceased to excite much curiosity.

To my great delight Zee avoided me, and evidently sought to excite my jealousy by marked attentions to a very handsome young An, who (though, as is the modest custom of the males when addressed by females, he answered with downcast eyes and blushing cheeks, and was demure and shy as young ladies new to the world are in most civilised countries, except England and America) was evidently much charmed by the tall Gy, and ready to falter a bashful "Yes" if she had actually proposed. Fervently hoping that she would, and more and more averse to the idea of reduction to a cinder after I had seen the rapidity with which a human body can be hurried into a pinch of dust, I amused myself by watching the manners of the other young people. I had the satisfaction of observing that Zee was no singular assertor of a female's most valued rights. Wherever I turned my eyes, or lent my ears, it seemed to me that the Gy was the wooing party, and the An the coy and reluctant one. The pretty innocent airs which an An gave himself on being thus courted, the dexterity with which he evaded direct answers to professions of attachment, or turned into jest the flattering compliments addressed to him, would have done honour to the most accomplished coquette. Both my male chaperons were subjected greatly to these seductive influences, and both acquitted themselves with wonderful honour to their tact and self-control.

I said to the elder son, who preferred mechanical employments to the management of a great property, and who was of an eminently philosophical temperament,—"I find it difficult to conceive how at your age, and with all the intoxicating effects on the senses, of music and lights and perfumes, you can be so cold to that impassioned young Gy who has just left you with tears in her eyes at your cruelty."

The young An replied with a sigh, "Gentle Tish, the greatest misfortune in life is to marry one Gy if you are in love with another."

"Oh! You are in love with another?"

"Alas! Yes."

"And she does not return your love?"

"I don't know. Sometimes a look, a tone, makes me hope so; but she has never plainly told me that she loves me."

"Have you not whispered in her own ear that you love her?"

"Fie! What are you thinking of? What world do you come from? Could I so betray the dignity of my sex? Could I be so un-Anly—so lost to shame, as to own love to a Gy who has not first owned hers to me?"

"Pardon: I was not quite aware that you pushed the modesty of your sex so far. But does no An ever say to a Gy, 'I love you,' till she says it first to him?"

"I can't say that no An has ever done so, but if he ever does, he is disgraced in the eyes of the Ana, and secretly despised by the Gy-ei. No Gy, well brought up, would listen to him; she would consider that he audaciously infringed on the rights of her sex, while outraging the modesty which dignifies his own. It is very provoking," continued the An, "for she whom I love has certainly courted no one else, and I cannot but think she likes me. Sometimes I suspect that she does not court me because she fears I would ask some unreasonable settlement as to the surrender of her rights. But if so, she cannot really love me, for where a Gy really loves she forgoes all rights."

"Is this young Gy present?"

"Oh yes. She sits yonder talking to my mother."

I looked in the direction to which my eyes were thus guided, and saw a Gy dressed in robes of bright red, which among this people is a sign that a Gy as yet prefers a single state. She wears gray, a neutral tint, to indicate that she is looking about for a spouse; dark purple if she wishes to intimate that she has made a choice; purple and orange when she is betrothed or married; light blue when she is divorced or a widow, and would marry again. Light blue is of course seldom seen.

Among a people where all are of so high a type of beauty, it is difficult to single out one as peculiarly handsome. My young friend's choice seemed to me to possess the average of good looks; but there was an expression in her face that pleased me more than did the faces of the young Gy-ei generally, because it looked less bold—less conscious of female rights. I observed that, while she talked to Bra, she glanced, from time to time, sidelong at my young friend.

"Courage," said I, "that young Gy loves you."

"Ay, but if she shall not say so, how am I the better for her love?"

"Your mother is aware of your attachment?"

"Perhaps so. I never owned it to her. It would be un-Anly to confide such weakness to a mother. I have told my father; he may have told it again to his wife."

"Will you permit me to quit you for a moment and glide behind your mother and your beloved? I am sure they are talking about you. Do not hesitate. I promise that I will not allow myself to be questioned till I rejoin you."

The young An pressed his hand on his heart, touched me lightly on the head, and allowed me to quit his side. I stole unobserved behind his mother and his beloved. I overheard their talk. Bra was speaking; said she, "There can be no doubt of this: either my son, who is of marriageable age, will be decoyed into marriage with one of his many suitors, or he will join those who emigrate to a distance and we shall see him no more. If you really care for him, my dear Lo, you should propose."

"I do care for him, Bra; but I doubt if I could really ever win his affections. He is fond of his inventions and timepieces; and I am not like Zee, but so dull that I fear I could not enter into his favourite pursuits, and then he would get tired of me, and at the end of three years divorce me, and I could never marry another—never."

"It is not necessary to know about timepieces to know how to be so necessary to the happiness of an An, who cares for timepieces, that he would rather give up the timepieces than divorce his Gy. You see, my dear Lo," continued Bra, "that precisely because we are the stronger sex, we rule the other provided we never show our strength. If you were superior to my son in making timepieces and automata, you should, as his wife, always let him suppose you thought him superior in that art to yourself. The An tacitly allows the pre-eminence of the Gy in all except his own special pursuit. But if she either excels him in that, or affects not to admire him for his proficiency in it, he will not love her very long; perhaps he may even divorce her. But where a Gy really loves, she soon learns to love all that the An does."

The young Gy made no answer to this address. She looked down musingly, then a smile crept over her lips, and she rose, still silent, and went through the crowd till she paused by the young An who loved her. I followed her steps, but discreetly stood at a little distance while I watched them. Somewhat to my surprise, till I recollected the coy tactics among the Ana, the lover seemed to receive her advances with an air of indifference. He even moved away, but she pursued his steps, and, a little time after, both spread their wings and vanished amid the luminous space above.

Just then I was accosted by the chief magistrate, who mingled with the crowd distinguished by no signs of deference or homage. It so happened that I had not seen this great dignitary since the day I had entered his dominions, and recalling Aph-Lin's words as to his terrible doubt whether or not I should be dissected, a shudder crept over me at the sight of his tranquil countenance.

"I hear much of you, stranger, from my son Taee," said the Tur, laying his hand politely on my bended head. "He is very fond of your society, and I trust you are not displeased with the customs of our people."

I muttered some unintelligible answer, which I intended to be an assurance of my gratitude for the kindness I had received from the Tur, and my admiration of his countrymen, but the dissecting-knife gleamed before my mind's eye and choked my utterance. A softer voice said, "My brother's friend must be dear to me." And looking up I saw a young Gy, who might be sixteen years old, standing beside the magistrate and gazing at me with a very benignant countenance.

She had not come to her full growth, and was scarcely taller than myself (viz., about feet 10 inches), and, thanks to that comparatively diminutive stature, I thought her the loveliest Gy I had hitherto seen. I suppose something in my eyes revealed that impression, for her countenance grew yet more benignant. "Taee tells me," she said, "that you have not yet learned to accustom yourself to wings. That grieves me, for I should have liked to fly with you."

"Alas!" I replied, "I can never hope to enjoy that happiness. I am assured by Zee that the safe use of wings is a hereditary gift, and it would take generations before one of my race could poise himself in the air like a bird." "Let not that thought vex you too much," replied this amiable Princess, "for, after all, there must come a day when Zee and myself must resign our wings forever. Perhaps when that day comes we might be glad if the An we chose was also without wings."

The Tur had left us, and was lost amongst the crowd. I began to feel at ease with Taee's charming sister, and rather startled her by the boldness of my compliment in replying, "that no An she could choose would ever use his wings to fly away from her." It is so against custom for an An to say such civil things to a Gy till she has declared her passion for him, and been accepted as his betrothed, that the young maiden stood quite dumbfounded for a few moments. Nevertheless she did not seem displeased. At last recovering herself, she invited me to accompany her into one of the less crowded rooms and listen to the songs of the birds. I followed her steps as she glided before me, and she led me into a chamber almost deserted. A fountain of naphtha was playing in the centre of the room; round it were ranged soft divans, and the walls of the room were open on one side to an aviary in which the birds were chanting their artful chorus. The Gy seated herself on one of the divans, and I placed myself at her side. "Taee tells me," she said, "that Aph-Lin has made it the law* of his house that you are not to be questioned as to the country you come from or the reason why you visit us. Is it so?"

* Literally "has said, In this house be it requested." Words synonymous with law, as implying forcible obligation, are avoided by this singular people. Even had it been decreed by the Tur that his College of Sages should dissect me, the decree would have ran blandly thus, — "Be it requested that, for the good of the community, the carnivorous Tish be requested to submit himself to dissection."

"It is."

"May I, at least, without sinning against that law, ask at least if the Gy-ei in your country are of the same pale colour as yourself, and no taller?"

"I do not think, O beautiful Gy, that I infringe the law of Aph-Lin, which is more binding on myself than any one, if I answer questions so innocent. The Gy-ei in my country are much fairer of hue than I am, and their average height is at least a head shorter than mine."

"They cannot then be so strong as the Ana amongst you? But I suppose their superior vril force makes up for such extraordinary disadvantage of size?"

"They do not profess the vril force as you know it. But still they are very powerful in my country, and an An has small chance of a happy life if he be not more or less governed by his Gy."

"You speak feelingly," said Taee's sister, in a tone of voice half sad, half petulant. "You are married, of course."

"No—certainly not."

"Nor betrothed?"

"Nor betrothed."

"Is it possible that no Gy has proposed to you?"

"In my country the Gy does not propose; the An speaks first."

"What a strange reversal of the laws of nature!" said the maiden, "and what want of modesty in your sex! But have you never proposed, never loved one Gy more than another?"

I felt embarrassed by these ingenious questionings, and said, "Pardon me, but I think we are beginning to infringe upon Aph-Lin's injunction. This much only will I answer, and then, I implore you, ask no more. I did once feel the preference you speak of; I did propose, and the Gy would willingly have accepted me, but her parents refused their consent."

"Parents! Do you mean seriously to tell me that parents can interfere with the choice of their daughters?"

"Indeed they can, and do very often."

"I should not like to live in that country," said the Gy simply; "but I hope you will never go back to it."

I bowed my head in silence. The Gy gently raised my face with her right hand, and looked into it tenderly. "Stay with us," she said; "stay with us, and be loved." What I might have answered, what dangers of becoming a cinder I might have encountered, I still trouble to think, when the light of the naphtha fountain was obscured by the shadow of wings; and Zee, flying though the open roof, alighted beside us. She said not a word, but, taking my arm with her mighty hand, she drew me away, as a mother draws a naughty child, and led me through the apartments to one of the corridors, on which, by the mechanism they generally prefer to stairs, we ascended to my own room. This gained, Zee breathed on my forehead, touched my breast with her staff, and I was instantly plunged into a profound sleep.

When I awoke some hours later, and heard the songs of the birds in the adjoining aviary, the remembrance of Taee's sister, her gentle looks and caressing words, vividly returned to me; and so impossible is it for one born and reared in our upper world's state of society to divest himself of ideas dictated by vanity and ambition, that I found myself instinctively building proud castles in the air.

"Tish though I be," thus ran my meditations—"Tish though I be, it is then clear that Zee is not the only Gy whom my appearance can captivate. Evidently I am loved by A PRINCESS, the first maiden of this land, the daughter of the absolute Monarch whose autocracy they so idly seek to disguise by the republican title of chief magistrate. But for the sudden swoop of that horrible Zee, this Royal Lady would have formally proposed to me; and though it may be very well for Aph-Lin, who is only a subordinate minister, a mere Commissioner of Light, to threaten me with destruction if I accept his daughter's hand, yet a Sovereign, whose word is law, could compel the community to abrogate any custom that forbids intermarriage with one of a strange race, and which in itself is a contradiction to their boasted equality of ranks.

"It is not to be supposed that his daughter, who spoke with such incredulous scorn of the interference of parents, would not have sufficient influence with her Royal Father to save me from the combustion to which Aph-Lin would condemn my form. And if I were exalted by such an alliance, who knows but what the Monarch might elect me as his successor? Why not? Few among this indolent race of philosophers like the burden of such greatness. All might be pleased to see the supreme power lodged in the hands of an accomplished stranger who has experience of other and livelier forms of existence; and once chosen, what reforms I would institute! What additions to the really pleasant but too monotonous life of this realm my familiarity with the civilised nations above ground would effect! I am fond of the sports of the field. Next to war, is not the chase a king's pastime? In what varieties of strange game does this nether world abound? How interesting to strike down creatures that were known above ground before the Deluge! But how? By that terrible vril, in which, from want of hereditary transmission, I could never be a proficient? No, but by a civilised handy breech-loader, which these ingenious mechanicians could not only make, but no doubt improve; nay, surely I saw one in the Museum. Indeed, as absolute king, I should discountenance vril altogether, except in cases of war. Apropos of war, it is perfectly absurd to stint a people so intelligent, so rich, so well armed, to a petty limit of territory sufficing for 10,000 or 12,000 families. Is not this restriction a mere philosophical crotchet, at variance with the aspiring element in human nature, such as has been partially, and with complete failure, tried in the upper world by the late Mr. Robert Owen? Of course one would not go to war with the neighbouring nations as well armed as one's own subjects; but then, what of those regions inhabited by races unacquainted with vril, and apparently resembling, in their democratic institutions, my American countrymen? One might invade them without offence to the vril nations, our allies, appropriate their territories, extending, perhaps, to the most distant regions of the nether earth, and thus rule over an empire in which the sun never sets. (I forgot, in my enthusiasm, that over those regions there was no sun to set). As for the fantastical notion against conceding fame or renown to an eminent individual, because, forsooth, bestowal of honours insures contest in the pursuit of them, stimulates angry passions, and mars the felicity of peace—it is opposed to the very elements, not only of the human, but of the brute creation, which are all, if tamable, participators in the sentiment of praise and emulation. What renown would be given to a king who thus extended his empire! I should be deemed a demigod." Thinking of that, the other fanatical notion of regulating this life by reference to one which, no doubt, we Christians firmly believe in, but never take into consideration, I resolved that enlightened philosophy compelled me to abolish a heathen religion so superstitiously at variance with modern thought and practical action. Musing over these various projects, I felt how much I should have liked at that moment to brighten my wits by a good glass of whiskey-and-water. Not that I am habitually a spirit-drinker, but certainly there are times when a little stimulant of alcoholic nature, taken with a cigar, enlivens the imagination. Yes; certainly among these herbs and fruits there would be a liquid from which one could extract a pleasant vinous alcohol; and with a steak cut off one of those elks (ah! what offence to science to reject the animal food which our first medical men agree in recommending to the gastric juices of mankind!) one would certainly pass a more exhilarating hour of repast. Then, too, instead of those antiquated dramas performed by childish amateurs, certainly, when I am king, I will introduce our modern opera and a 'corps de ballet,' for which one might find, among the nations I shall conquer, young females of less formidable height and thews than the Gy-ei—not armed with vril, and not insisting upon one's marrying them.

I was so completely rapt in these and similar reforms, political, social, and moral, calculated to bestow on the people of the nether world the blessings of a civilisation known to the races of the upper, that I did not perceive that Zee had entered the chamber till I heard a deep sigh, and, raising my eyes, beheld her standing by my couch.

I need not say that, according to the manners of this people, a Gy can, without indecorum, visit an An in his chamber, although an An would be considered forward and immodest to the last degree if he entered the chamber of a Gy without previously obtaining her permission to do so. Fortunately I was in the full habiliments I had worn when Zee had deposited me on the couch. Nevertheless I felt much irritated, as well as shocked, by her visit, and asked in a rude tone what she wanted.

"Speak gently, beloved one, I entreat you," said she, "for I am very unhappy. I have not slept since we parted."

"A due sense of your shameful conduct to me as your father's guest might well suffice to banish sleep from your eyelids. Where was the affection you pretend to have for me, where was even that politeness on which the Vril-ya pride themselves, when, taking advantage alike of that physical strength in which your sex, in this extraordinary region, excels our own, and of those detestable and unhallowed powers which the agencies of vril invest in your eyes and finger-ends, you exposed me to humiliation before your assembled visitors, before Her Royal Highness—I mean, the daughter of your own chief magistrate,—carrying me off to bed like a naughty infant, and plunging me into sleep, without asking my consent?"

"Ungrateful! Do you reproach me for the evidences of my love? Can you think that, even if unstung by the jealousy which attends upon love till it fades away in blissful trust when we know that the heart we have wooed is won, I could be indifferent to the perils to which the audacious overtures of that silly little child might expose you?" "Hold! Since you introduce the subject of perils, it perhaps does not misbecome me to say that my most imminent perils come from yourself, or at least would come if I believed in your love and accepted your addresses. Your father has told me plainly that in that case I should be consumed into a cinder with as little compunction as if I were the reptile whom Taee blasted into ashes with the flash of his wand."

"Do not let that fear chill your heart to me," exclaimed Zee, dropping on her knees and absorbing my right hand in the space of her ample palm. "It is true, indeed, that we two cannot wed as those of the same race wed; true that the love between us must be pure as that which, in our belief, exists between lovers who reunite in the new life beyond that boundary at which the old life ends. But is it not happiness enough to be together, wedded in mind and in heart? Listen: I have just left my father. He consents to our union on those terms. I have sufficient influence with the College of Sages to insure their request to the Tur not to interfere with the free choice of a Gy; provided that her wedding with one of another race be but the wedding of souls. Oh, think you that true love needs ignoble union? It is not that I yearn only to be by your side in this life, to be part and parcel of your joys and sorrows here: I ask here for a tie which will bind us for ever and for ever in the world of immortals. Do you reject me?"

As she spoke, she knelt, and the whole character of her face was changed; nothing of sternness left to its grandeur; a divine light, as that of an immortal, shining out from its human beauty. But she rather awed me as an angel than moved me as a woman, and after an embarrassed pause, I faltered forth evasive expressions of gratitude, and sought, as delicately as I could, to point out how humiliating would be my position amongst her race in the light of a husband who might never be permitted the name of father.

"But," said Zee, "this community does not constitute the whole world. No; nor do all the populations comprised in the league of the Vril-ya. For thy sake I will renounce my country and my people. We will fly together to some region where thou shalt be safe. I am strong enough to bear thee on my wings across the deserts that intervene. I am skilled enough to cleave open, amidst the rocks, valleys in which to build our home. Solitude and a hut with thee would be to me society and the universe. Or wouldst thou return to thine own world, above the surface of this, exposed to the uncertain seasons, and lit but by the changeful orbs which constitute by thy description the fickle character of those savage regions? I so, speak the word, and I will force the way for thy return, so that I am thy companion there, though, there as here, but partner of thy soul, and fellow traveller with thee to the world in which there is no parting and no death."

I could not but be deeply affected by the tenderness, at once so pure and so impassioned, with which these words were uttered, and in a voice that would have rendered musical the roughest sounds in the rudest tongue. And for a moment it did occur to me that I might avail myself of Zee's agency to effect a safe and speedy return to the upper world. But a very brief space for reflection sufficed to show me how dishonourable and base a return for such devotion it would be to allure thus away, from her own people and a home in which I had been so hospitably treated, a creature to whom our world would be so abhorrent, and for whose barren, if spiritual love, I could not reconcile myself to renounce the more human affection of mates less exalted above my erring self. With this sentiment of duty towards the Gy combined another of duty towards the whole race I belonged to. Could I venture to introduce into the upper world a being so formidably gifted—a being that with a movement of her staff could in less than an hour reduce New York and its glorious Koom-Posh into a pinch of snuff? Rob her of her staff, with her science she could easily construct another; and with the deadly lightnings that armed the slender engine her whole frame was charged. If thus dangerous to the cities and populations of the whole upper earth, could she be a safe companion to myself in case her affection should be subjected to change or embittered by jealousy? These thoughts, which it takes so many words to express, passed rapidly through my brain and decided my answer.

"Zee," I said, in the softest tones I could command and pressing respectful lips on the hand into whose clasp mine vanished—"Zee, I can find no words to say how deeply I am touched, and how highly I am honoured, by a love so disinterested and self-immolating. My best return to it is perfect frankness. Each nation has its customs. The customs of yours do not allow you to wed me; the customs of mine are equally opposed to such a union between those of races so widely differing. On the other hand, though not deficient in courage among my own people, or amid dangers with which I am familiar, I cannot, without a shudder of horror, think of constructing a bridal home in the heart of some dismal chaos, with all the elements of nature, fire and water, and mephitic gases, at war with each other, and with the probability that at some moment, while you were busied in cleaving rocks or conveying vril into lamps, I should be devoured by a krek which your operations disturbed from its hiding-place. I, a mere Tish, do not deserve the love of a Gy, so brilliant, so learned, so potent as yourself. Yes, I do not deserve that love, for I cannot return it."

Zee released my hand, rose to her feet, and turned her face away to hide her emotions; then she glided noiselessly along the room, and paused at the threshold. Suddenly, impelled as by a new thought, she returned to my side and said, in a whispered tone,—

"You told me you would speak with perfect frankness. With perfect frankness, then, answer me this question. If you cannot love me, do you love another?"

"Certainly, I do not."

"You do not love Taee's sister?"

"I never saw her before last night." "That is no answer. Love is swifter than vril. You hesitate to tell me. Do not think it is only jealousy that prompts me to caution you. If the Tur's daughter should declare love to you—if in her ignorance she confides to her father any preference that may justify his belief that she will woo you, he will have no option but to request your immediate destruction, as he is specially charged with the duty of consulting the good of the community, which could not allow the daughter of the Vril-ya to wed a son of the Tish-a, in that sense of marriage which does not confine itself to union of the souls. Alas! there would then be for you no escape. She has no strength of wing to uphold you through the air; she has no science wherewith to make a home in the wilderness. Believe that here my friendship speaks, and that my jealousy is silent."

With these words Zee left me. And recalling those words, I thought no more of succeeding to the throne of the Vril-ya, or of the political, social, and moral reforms I should institute in the capacity of Absolute Sovereign.

Chapter XXVI.

After the conversation with Zee just recorded, I fell into a profound melancholy. The curious interest with which I had hitherto examined the life and habits of this marvellous community was at an end. I could not banish from my mind the consciousness that I was among a people who, however kind and courteous, could destroy me at any moment without scruple or compunction. The virtuous and peaceful life of the people which, while new to me, had seemed so holy a contrast to the contentions, the passions, the vices of the upper world, now began to oppress me with a sense of dulness and monotony. Even the serene tranquility of the lustrous air preyed on my spirits. I longed for a change, even to winter, or storm, or darkness. I began to feel that, whatever our dreams of perfectibility, our restless aspirations towards a better, and higher, and calmer, sphere of being, we, the mortals of the upper world, are not trained or fitted to enjoy for long the very happiness of which we dream or to which we aspire.

Now, in this social state of the Vril-ya, it was singular to mark how it contrived to unite and to harmonise into one system nearly all the objects which the various philosophers of the upper world have placed before human hopes as the ideals of a Utopian future. It was a state in which war, with all its calamities, was deemed impossible,—a state in which the freedom of all and each was secured to the uttermost degree, without one of those animosities which make freedom in the upper world depend on the perpetual strife of hostile parties. Here the corruption which debases democracies was as unknown as the discontents which undermine the thrones of monarchies. Equality here was not a name; it was a reality. Riches were not persecuted, because they were not envied. Here those problems connected with the labours of a working class, hitherto insoluble above ground, and above ground conducing to such bitterness between classes, were solved by a process the simplest,—a distinct and separate working class was dispensed with altogether. Mechanical inventions, constructed on the principles that baffled my research to ascertain, worked by an agency infinitely more powerful and infinitely more easy of management than aught we have yet extracted from electricity or steam, with the aid of children whose strength was never overtasked, but who loved their employment as sport and pastime, sufficed to create a Public-wealth so devoted to the general use that not a grumbler was ever heard of. The vices that rot our cities here had no footing. Amusements abounded, but they were all innocent. No merry-makings conduced to intoxication, to riot, to disease. Love existed, and was ardent in pursuit, but its object, once secured, was faithful. The adulterer, the profligate, the harlot, were phenomena so unknown in this commonwealth, that even to find the words by which they were designated one would have had to search throughout an obsolete literature composed thousands of years before. They who have been students of theoretical philosophies above ground, know that all these strange departures from civilised life do but realise ideas which have been broached, canvassed, ridiculed, contested for; sometimes partially tried, and still put forth in fantastic books, but have never come to practical result. Nor were these all the steps towards theoretical perfectibility which this community had made. It had been the sober belief of Descartes that the life of man could be prolonged, not, indeed, on this earth, to eternal duration, but to what he called the age of the patriarchs, and modestly defined to be from 100 to 150 years average length. Well, even this dream of sages was here fulfilled—nay, more than fulfilled; for the vigour of middle life was preserved even after the term of a century was passed. With this longevity was combined a greater blessing than itself—that of continuous health. Such diseases as befell the race were removed with ease by scientific applications of that agency—life-giving as life-destroying—which is inherent in vril. Even this idea is not unknown above ground, though it has generally been confined to enthusiasts or charlatans, and emanates from confused notions about mesmerism, odic force, &c. Passing by such trivial contrivances as wings, which every schoolboy knows has been tried and found wanting, from the mythical or pre-historical period, I proceed to that very delicate question, urged of late as essential to the perfect happiness of our human species by the two most disturbing and potential influences on upper-ground society,—Womankind and Philosophy. I mean, the Rights of Women.

Now, it is allowed by jurisprudists that it is idle to talk of rights where there are not corresponding powers to enforce them; and above ground, for some reason or other, man, in his physical force, in the use of weapons offensive and defensive, when it come to positive personal contest, can, as a rule of general application, master women. But among this people there can be no doubt about the rights of women, because, as I have before said, the Gy, physically speaking, is bigger and stronger than the An; and her will being also more resolute than his, and will being essential to the direction of the vril force, she can bring to bear upon him, more potently than he on herself, the mystical agency which art can extract from the occult properties of nature. Therefore all that our female philosophers above ground contend for as to rights of women, is conceded as a matter of course in this happy commonwealth. Besides such physical powers, the Gy-ei have (at least in youth) a keen desire for accomplishments and learning which exceeds that of the male; and thus they are the scholars, the professors—the learned portion, in short, of the community.

Of course, in this state of society the female establishes, as I have shown, her most valued privilege, that of choosing and courting her wedding partner. Without that privilege she would despise all the others. Now, above ground, we should not unreasonably apprehend that a female, thus potent and thus privileged, when she had fairly hunted us down and married us, would be very imperious and tyrannical. Not so with the Gy-ei: once married, the wings once suspended, and more amiable, complacent, docile mates, more sympathetic, more sinking their loftier capacities into the study of their husbands' comparatively frivolous tastes and whims, no poet could conceive in his visions of conjugal bliss. Lastly, among the more important characteristics of the Vril-ya, as distinguished from our mankind—lastly, and most important on the bearings of their life and the peace of their commonwealths, is their universal agreement in the existence of a merciful beneficent Diety, and of a future world to the duration of which a century or two are moments too brief to waste upon thoughts of fame and power and avarice; while with that agreement is combined another—viz., since they can know nothing as to the nature of that Diety beyond the fact of His supreme goodness, nor of that future world beyond the fact of its felicitous existence, so their reason forbids all angry disputes on insoluble questions.

Thus they secure for that state in the bowels of the earth what no community ever secured under the light of the stars—all the blessings and consolations of a religion without any of the evils and calamities which are engendered by strife between one religion and another.

It would be, then, utterly impossible to deny that the state of existence among the Vril-ya is thus, as a whole, immeasurably more felicitous than that of super-terrestrial races, and, realising the dreams of our most sanguine philanthropists, almost approaches to a poet's conception of some angelical order. And yet, if you would take a thousand of the best and most philosophical of human beings you could find in London, Paris, Berlin, New York, or even Boston, and place them as citizens in the beatified community, my belief is, that in less than a year they would either die of ennui, or attempt some revolution by which they would militate against the good of the community, and be burnt into cinders at the request of the Tur.

Certainly I have no desire to insinuate, through the medium of this narrative, any ignorant disparagement of the race to which I belong. I have, on the contrary, endeavoured to make it clear that the principles which regulate the social system of the Vril-ya forbid them to produce those individual examples of human greatness which adorn the annals of the upper world. Where there are no wars there can be no Hannibal, no Washington, no Jackson, no Sheridan;—where states are so happy that they fear no danger and desire no change, they cannot give birth to a Demosthenes, a Webster, a Sumner, a Wendell Holmes, or a Butler; and where a society attains to a moral standard, in which there are no crimes and no sorrows from which tragedy can extract its aliment of pity and sorrow, no salient vices or follies on which comedy can lavish its mirthful satire, it has lost the chance of producing a Shakespeare, or a Moliere, or a Mrs. Beecher-Stowe. But if I have no desire to disparage my fellow-men above ground in showing how much the motives that impel the energies and ambition of individuals in a society of contest and struggle—become dormant or annulled in a society which aims at securing for the aggregate the calm and innocent felicity which we presume to be the lot of beatified immortals; neither, on the other hand, have I the wish to represent the commonwealths of the Vril-ya as an ideal form of political society, to the attainment of which our own efforts of reform should be directed. On the contrary, it is because we have so combined, throughout the series of ages, the elements which compose human character, that it would be utterly impossible for us to adopt the modes of life, or to reconcile our passions to the modes of thought among the Vril-ya,—that I arrived at the conviction that this people—though originally not only of our human race, but, as seems to me clear by the roots of their language, descended from the same ancestors as the Great Aryan family, from which in varied streams has flowed the dominant civilisation of the world; and having, according to their myths and their history, passed through phases of society familiar to ourselves,—had yet now developed into a distinct species with which it was impossible that any community in the upper world could amalgamate: and that if they ever emerged from these nether recesses into the light of day, they would, according to their own traditional persuasions of their ultimate destiny, destroy and replace our existent varieties of man.

It may, indeed, be said, since more than one Gy could be found to conceive a partiality for so ordinary a type of our super-terrestrial race as myself, that even if the Vril-ya did appear above ground, we might be saved from extermination by intermixture of race. But this is too sanguine a belief. Instances of such 'mesalliance' would be as rare as those of intermarriage between the Anglo-Saxon emigrants and the Red Indians. Nor would time be allowed for the operation of familiar intercourse. The Vril-ya, on emerging, induced by the charm of a sunlit heaven to form their settlements above ground, would commence at once the work of destruction, seize upon the territories already cultivated, and clear off, without scruple, all the inhabitants who resisted that invasion. And considering their contempt for the institutions of Koom-Posh or Popular Government, and the pugnacious valour of my beloved countrymen, I believe that if the Vril-ya first appeared in free America—as, being the choicest portion of the habitable earth, they would doubtless be induced to do—and said, "This quarter of the globe we take, Citizens of a Koom-Posh, make way for the development of species in the Vril-ya," my brave compatriots would show fight, and not a soul of them would be left in this life, to rally round the Stars and Stripes, at the end of a week.

I now saw but little of Zee, save at meals, when the family assembled, and she was then reserved and silent. My apprehensions of danger from an affection I had so little encouraged or deserved, therefore, now faded away, but my dejection continued to increase. I pined for escape to the upper world, but I racked my brains in vain for any means to effect it. I was never permitted to wander forth alone, so that I could not even visit the spot on which I had alighted, and see if it were possible to reascend to the mine. Nor even in the Silent Hours, when the household was locked in sleep, could I have let myself down from the lofty floor in which my apartment was placed. I knew not how to command the automata who stood mockingly at my beck beside the wall, nor could I ascertain the springs by which were set in movement the platforms that supplied the place of stairs. The knowledge how to avail myself of these contrivances had been purposely withheld from me. Oh, that I could but have learned the use of wings, so freely here at the service of every infant, then I might have escaped from the casement, regained the rocks, and buoyed myself aloft through the chasm of which the perpendicular sides forbade place for human footing!

Chapter XXVII.

One day, as I sat alone and brooding in my chamber, Taee flew in at the open window and alighted on the couch beside me. I was always pleased with the visits of a child, in whose society, if humbled, I was less eclipsed than in that of Ana who had completed their education and matured their understanding. And as I was permitted to wander forth with him for my companion, and as I longed to revisit the spot in which I had descended into the nether world, I hastened to ask him if he were at leisure for a stroll beyond the streets of the city. His countenance seemed to me graver than usual as he replied, "I came hither on purpose to invite you forth."

We soon found ourselves in the street, and had not got far from the house when we encountered five or six young Gy-ei, who were returning from the fields with baskets full of flowers, and chanting a song in chorus as they walked. A young Gy sings more often than she talks. They stopped on seeing us, accosting Taee with familiar kindness, and me with the courteous gallantry which distinguishes the Gy-ei in their manner towards our weaker sex.

And here I may observe that, though a virgin Gy is so frank in her courtship to the individual she favours, there is nothing that approaches to that general breadth and loudness of manner which those young ladies of the Anglo-Saxon race, to whom the distinguished epithet of 'fast' is accorded, exhibit towards young gentlemen whom they do not profess to love. No; the bearing of the Gy-ei towards males in ordinary is very much that of high-bred men in the gallant societies of the upper world towards ladies whom they respect but do not woo; deferential, complimentary, exquisitely polished—what we should call 'chivalrous.'

Certainly I was a little put out by the number of civil things addressed to my 'amour propre,' which were said to me by those courteous young Gy-ei. In the world I came from, a man would have thought himself aggrieved, treated with irony, 'chaffed' (if so vulgar a slang word may be allowed on the authority of the popular novelists who use it so freely), when one fair Gy complimented me on the freshness of my complexion, another on the choice of colours in my dress, a third, with a sly smile, on the conquests I had made at Aph-Lin's entertainment. But I knew already that all such language was what the French call 'banal,' and did but express in the female mouth, below earth, that sort of desire to pass for amiable with the opposite sex which, above earth, arbitrary custom and hereditary transmission demonstrate by the mouth of the male. And just as a high-bred young lady, above earth, habituated to such compliments, feels that she cannot, without impropriety, return them, nor evince any great satisfaction at receiving them; so I who had learned polite manners at the house of so wealthy and dignified a Minister of that nation, could but smile and try to look pretty in bashfully disclaiming the compliments showered upon me. While we were thus talking, Taee's sister, it seems, had seen us from the upper rooms of the Royal Palace at the entrance of the town, and, precipitating herself on her wings, alighted in the midst of the group.

Singling me out, she said, though still with the inimitable deference of manner which I have called 'chivalrous,' yet not without a certain abruptness of tone which, as addressed to the weaker sex, Sir Philip Sydney might have termed 'rustic,' "Why do you never come to see us?" While I was deliberating on the right answer to give to this unlooked-for question, Taee said quickly and sternly, "Sister, you forget—the stranger is of my sex. It is not for persons of my sex, having due regard for reputation and modesty, to lower themselves by running after the society of yours."

This speech was received with evident approval by the young Gy-ei in general; but Taee's sister looked greatly abashed. Poor thing!— and a PRINCESS too!

Just at this moment a shadow fell on the space between me and the group; and, turning round, I beheld the chief magistrate coming close upon us, with the silent and stately pace peculiar to the Vril-ya. At the sight of his countenance, the same terror which had seized me when I first beheld it returned. On that brow, in those eyes, there was that same indefinable something which marked the being of a race fatal to our own—that strange expression of serene exemption from our common cares and passions, of conscious superior power, compassionate and inflexible as that of a judge who pronounces doom. I shivered, and, inclining low, pressed the arm of my child-friend, and drew him onward silently. The Tur placed himself before our path, regarded me for a moment without speaking, then turned his eye quietly on his daughter's face, and, with a grave salutation to her and the other Gy-ei, went through the midst of the group,—still without a word.

Chapter XXVIII.

When Taee and I found ourselves alone on the broad road that lay between the city and the chasm through which I had descended into this region beneath the light of the stars and sun, I said under my breath, "Child and friend, there is a look in your father's face which appals me. I feel as if, in its awful tranquillity, I gazed upon death."

Taee did not immediately reply. He seemed agitated, and as if debating with himself by what words to soften some unwelcome intelligence. At last he said, "None of the Vril-ya fear death: do you?"

"The dread of death is implanted in the breasts of the race to which I belong. We can conquer it at the call of duty, of honour, of love. We can die for a truth, for a native land, for those who are dearer to us than ourselves. But if death do really threaten me now and here, where are such counteractions to the natural instinct which invests with awe and terror the contemplation of severance between soul and body?"

Taee looked surprised, but there was great tenderness in his voice as he replied, "I will tell my father what you say. I will entreat him to spare your life."

"He has, then, already decreed to destroy it?"

"'Tis my sister's fault or folly," said Taee, with some petulance. "But she spoke this morning to my father; and, after she had spoken, he summoned me, as a chief among the children who are commissioned to destroy such lives as threaten the community, and he said to me, 'Take thy vril staff, and seek the stranger who has made himself dear to thee. Be his end painless and prompt.'"

"And," I faltered, recoiling from the child—"and it is, then, for my murder that thus treacherously thou hast invited me forth? No, I cannot believe it. I cannot think thee guilty of such a crime."

"It is no crime to slay those who threaten the good of the community; it would be a crime to slay the smallest insect that cannot harm us."

"If you mean that I threaten the good of the community because your sister honours me with the sort of preference which a child may feel for a strange plaything, it is not necessary to kill me. Let me return to the people I have left, and by the chasm through which I descended. With a slight help from you I might do so now. You, by the aid of your wings, could fasten to the rocky ledge within the chasm the cord that you found, and have no doubt preserved. Do but that; assist me but to the spot from which I alighted, and I vanish from your world for ever, and as surely as if I were among the dead."

"The chasm through which you descended! Look round; we stand now on the very place where it yawned. What see you? Only solid rock. The chasm was closed, by the orders of Aph-Lin, as soon as communication between him and yourself was established in your trance, and he learned from your own lips the nature of the world from which you came. Do you not remember when Zee bade me not question you as to yourself or your race? On quitting you that day, Aph-Lin accosted me, and said, 'No path between the stranger's home and ours should be left unclosed, or the sorrow and evil of his home may descend to ours. Take with thee the children of thy band, smite the sides of the cavern with your vril staves till the fall of their fragments fills up every chink through which a gleam of our lamps could force its way.'"

As the child spoke, I stared aghast at the blind rocks before me. Huge and irregular, the granite masses, showing by charred discolouration where they had been shattered, rose from footing to roof-top; not a cranny!

"All hope, then, is gone," I murmured, sinking down on the craggy wayside, "and I shall nevermore see the sun." I covered my face with my hands, and prayed to Him whose presence I had so often forgotten when the heavens had declared His handiwork. I felt His presence in the depths of the nether earth, and amidst the world of the grave. I looked up, taking comfort and courage from my prayers, and, gazing with a quiet smile into the face of the child, said, "Now, if thou must slay me, strike."

Taee shook his head gently. "Nay," he said, "my father's request is not so formally made as to leave me no choice. I will speak with him, and may prevail to save thee. Strange that thou shouldst have that fear of death which we thought was only the instinct of the inferior creatures, to whom the convictions of another life has not been vouchsafed. With us, not an infant knows such a fear. Tell me, my dear Tish," he continued after a little pause, "would it reconcile thee more to departure from this form of life to that form which lies on the other side of the moment called 'death,' did I share thy journey? If so, I will ask my father whether it be allowable for me to go with thee. I am one of our generation destined to emigrate, when of age for it, to some regions unknown within this world. I would just as soon emigrate now to regions unknown, in another world. The All-Good is no less there than here. Where is he not?"

"Child," said I, seeing by Taee's countenance that he spoke in serious earnest, "it is crime in thee to slay me; it were a crime not less in me to say, 'Slay thyself.' The All-Good chooses His own time to give us life, and his own time to take it away. Let us go back. If, on speaking with thy father, he decides on my death, give me the longest warning in thy power, so that I may pass the interval in self-preparation."

Chapter XXIX.

In the midst of those hours set apart for sleep and constituting the night of the Vril-ya, I was awakened from the disturbed slumber into which I had not long fallen, by a hand on my shoulder. I started and beheld Zee standing beside me. "Hush," she said in a whisper; "let no one hear us. Dost thou think that I have ceased to watch over thy safety because I could not win thy love? I have seen Taee. He has not prevailed with his father, who had meanwhile conferred with the three sages who, in doubtful matters, he takes into council, and by their advice he has ordained thee to perish when the world re-awakens to life. I will save thee. Rise and dress."

Zee pointed to a table by the couch on which I saw the clothes I had worn on quitting the upper world, and which I had exchanged subsequently for the more picturesque garments of the Vril-ya. The young Gy then moved towards the casement and stepped into the balcony, while hastily and wonderingly I donned my own habiliments. When I joined her on the balcony, her face was pale and rigid. Taking me by the hand, she said softly, "See how brightly the art of the Vril-ya has lighted up the world in which they dwell. To-morrow the world will be dark to me." She drew me back into the room without waiting for my answer, thence into the corridor, from which we descended into the hall. We passed into the deserted streets and along the broad upward road which wound beneath the rocks. Here, where there is neither day nor night, the Silent Hours are unutterably solemn—the vast space illumined by mortal skill is so wholly without the sight and stir of mortal life. Soft as were our footsteps, their sounds vexed the ear, as out of harmony with the universal repose. I was aware in my own mind, though Zee said it not, that she had decided to assist my return to the upper world, and that we were bound towards the place from which I had descended. Her silence infected me and commanded mine. And now we approached the chasm. It had been re-opened; not presenting, indeed, the same aspect as when I had emerged from it, but through that closed wall of rock before which I had last stood with Taee, a new clift had been riven, and along its blackened sides still glimmered sparks and smouldered embers. My upward gaze could not, however, penetrate more than a few feet into the darkness of the hollow void, and I stood dismayed, and wondering how that grim ascent was to be made.

Zee divined my doubt. "Fear not," said she, with a faint smile; "your return is assured. I began this work when the Silent Hours commenced, and all else were asleep; believe that I did not paused till the path back into thy world was clear. I shall be with thee a little while yet. We do not part until thou sayest, 'Go, for I need thee no more.'"

My heart smote me with remorse at these words. "Ah!" I exclaimed, "would that thou wert of my race or I of thine, then I should never say, 'I need thee no more.'"

"I bless thee for those words, and I shall remember them when thou art gone," answered the Gy, tenderly.

During this brief interchange of words, Zee had turned away from me, her form bent and her head bowed over her breast. Now, she rose to the full height of her grand stature, and stood fronting me. While she had been thus averted from my gaze, she had lighted up the circlet that she wore round her brow, so that it blazed as if it were a crown of stars. Not only her face and her form, but the atmosphere around, were illumined by the effulgence of the diadem.

"Now," said she, "put thine arm around me for the first and last time. Nay, thus; courage, and cling firm."

As she spoke her form dilated, the vast wings expanded. Clinging to her, I was borne aloft through the terrible chasm. The starry light from her forehead shot around and before us through the darkness. Brightly and steadfastly, and swiftly as an angel may soar heavenward with the soul it rescues from the grave, went the flight of the Gy, till I heard in the distance the hum of human voices, the sounds of human toil. We halted on the flooring of one of the galleries of the mine, and beyond, in the vista, burned the dim, feeble lamps of the miners. Then I released my hold. The Gy kissed me on my forehead, passionately, but as with a mother's passion, and said, as the tears gushed from her eyes, "Farewell for ever. Thou wilt not let me go into thy world—

thou canst never return to mine. Ere our household shake off slumber, the rocks will have again closed over the chasm not to be re-opened by me, nor perhaps by others, for ages yet unguessed. Think of me sometimes, and with kindness. When I reach the life that lies beyond this speck in time, I shall look round for thee. Even there, the world consigned to thyself and thy people may have rocks and gulfs which divide it from that in which I rejoin those of my race that have gone before, and I may be powerless to cleave way to regain thee as I have cloven way to lose."

Her voice ceased. I heard the swan-like sough of her wings, and saw the rays of her starry diadem receding far and farther through the gloom.

I sate myself down for some time, musing sorrowfully; then I rose and took my way with slow footsteps towards the place in which I heard the sounds of men. The miners I encountered were strange to me, of another nation than my own. They turned to look at me with some surprise, but finding that I could not answer their brief questions in their own language, they returned to their work and suffered me to pass on unmolested. In fine, I regained the mouth of the mine, little troubled by other interrogatories;—save those of a friendly official to whom I was known, and luckily he was too busy to talk much with me. I took care not to return to my former lodging, but hastened that very day to quit a neighbourhood where I could not long have escaped inquiries to which I could have given no satisfactory answers. I regained in safety my own country, in which I have been long peacefully settled, and engaged in practical business, till I retired on a competent fortune, three years ago. I have been little invited and little tempted to talk of the rovings and adventures of my youth. Somewhat disappointed, as most men are, in matters connected with household love and domestic life, I often think of the young Gy as I sit alone at night, and wonder how I could have rejected such a love, no matter what dangers attended it, or by what conditions it was restricted. Only, the more I think of a people calmly developing, in regions excluded from our sight and deemed uninhabitable by our sages, powers surpassing our most disciplined modes of force, and virtues to which our life, social and political, becomes antagonistic in proportion as our civilisation advances,—the more devoutly I pray that ages may yet elapse before there emerge into sunlight our inevitable destroyers. Being, however, frankly told by my physician that I am afflicted by a complaint which, though it gives little pain and no perceptible notice of its encroachments, may at any moment be fatal, I have thought it my duty to my fellow-men to place on record these forewarnings of The Coming Race.